ORIGINS
OF
DREAMS

ISBN (paperback): 978-1-968919-09-2
ISBN (ebook): 978-1-968919-10-8

ARMINLEAR

Armin Lear Press, Inc.
215 W Riverside Drive, #4362
Estes Park, CO 80517

ORIGINS
OF
DREAMS

HOW AND WHY WE DREAM

SHLOMO YAKOBOVITS

ARMINLEAR

PREFACE

One night in 1945, a 17-year-old girl named Rivka climbed into bed in the Displaced Persons camp in Zeilsheim, Germany. She was about to sail to Sweden for a new life. The girl, who had spent her childhood fleeing, languishing in a death camp, wandering, and escaping death, just wanted to sleep. In the past few years, sleep had been hard to come by, both when fleeing for her life and during her time in the Bergen-Belsen concentration camp.

Sleep was always the most dangerous time of the day, when the body sank into the depths and gathered a bit of strength. In a world where human beings had lost all humaneness and death waited around every corner, dreams were the farthest thing from her mind. That night Rivka dreamed a dream. In it, her father, who had been murdered several years before, appeared to her, asking her not to go to Sweden, but instead to the Holy Land. Rivka awoke from the dream and, in one daring step, decided to make it come true. She parted from the traveling companion she had befriended and set off on a journey into the unknown.

Some 44 years after that dream, I arrived in the world one early morning. My mother – Rivka's daughter – named after the father who appeared in the dream, brought me into the world. One dream, which she could have dismissed as just another ordinary dream, changed Rivka's life and, in time, my life and that of my family. Thanks to that dream, my parents, my family, and I continue to dream.

What is it about dreams that cloaks them in mysticism and mystery, even though we encounter them regularly? How is it that dreams pass by us and we don't attach any significance to them? Can dreams teach us about ourselves? As with anything important and mysterious, everyone seeks to appropriate dreams into his or her own world.

I decided to set out on a journey in pursuit of dreams. Rather than settling for only one world, I decided to examine dreams as portrayed in various worlds, investigating our bodies, minds, and souls along the way. My quest has taken me into the realms of science, philosophy, psychology, history, the Bible, and Jewish mysticism.

I encountered treasures usually reserved mainly for scientists, philosophers, psychologists, historians, and rabbis. Each one holds real secrets, helping us understand dreams better. Like a 1,000-piece jigsaw puzzle, I started with the frame. After that, I began to focus on colors, smells, and ideas. I also focused on dreamers in scientific journals, sleep labs, and many books, until I gradually began to piece together the whole puzzle – which is my book and my dream that you have before you.

Ready to start dreaming together?

CONTENTS

1

ON THE HISTORY AND CULTURE OF DREAMS

PREFACE TO A JOURNEY THROUGH TIME

There is no one who doesn't dream. Even blind people dream; there are dreams in which a blind person undergoes a visual experience, just like a seeing person (seeing dreams), and there are diagnostic dreams, in which blind people's dreams reflect their experience of being blind, along with other beliefs and symbols. Studies show that in dreams, blind people gain encouragement and feel free, and these dreams help create integration between the visual dream and the blind reality.

In recent years it has also been found that animals, like humans, also dream. In various studies, researchers have succeeded in proving that monkeys, cats, and dogs also dream, during which the animals, like humans, undergo rapid eye movement. Dr. Stanley Koren of Columbia University believes that the phenomenon of dreaming is widespread among mammals, although it is possible to distinguish among various qualities of dreams. Researchers estimate that dream sleep has existed among all land mammals since the time they appeared on Earth, about 150 million years ago.

We are asleep for almost a third of our lives, and a significant portion of our sleep is dedicated to dreaming. According to a calculation by Tenzin Wangyal Rinpoche in his book *The Tibetan Yogas of Dream and Sleep*, each of us spends the equivalent of 25 to 35 years in dreams. Have you ever thought about how much of your life, in which you want to accomplish as much as possible, is invested in dreams?

So how many dreams do we dream over the course of our lives? A rough calculation by the British psychologist Richard Wiseman shows that today, the average person dreams close to 110,000 dreams, of which 85,000 are in the stages between adolescence and old age. An impressive output, despite the lack of popularity we ascribe to dreams, and the way every morning we largely forget the dreams of the preceding night.

Dreaming is gaining momentum throughout the world. Sleep and dream research labs can be found in almost every city, and a 2017 article in *The New York Times* reported that people worldwide spend more than $50 billion a year on sleep and dream aids. Many dreamers choose to recount their dreams, see them as a model and as inspiration, and share them with others. The psychologists Adam Schneider and G. William Domhoff, who established the "Dream Bank"[1] where over 20,000 dreams have been collected, have presented a range of possibilities for interpreting dreams and locating identical dreams. There are other internet sites where people choose to share their dreams, such as Dreamboard and DreamsCloud. Dreams have again taken center stage as they did in ancient times.

---

1   https://www.dreambank.net

One interesting thing is that we *all* dream. Yes, that's quite a challenge, taking into account the fact that the content of dreams varies from person to person, from place to place, from period to period. Nevertheless, we all see a sort of "movie" every night, which is directly or indirectly influenced by our conscious mind, our subconscious, and the experiences we have collected – good or bad – throughout our lives. Fasten your seatbelts because the journey to dreams, like all journeys, starts at the beginning.

THE HISTORY OF DREAMS

We have never stopped dreaming. The transition from wakefulness to dreaming, from reality to imagination, has always been accompanied by a certain ambiguity. Moreover, the similarity between sleep and death has occupied humanity since the dawn of history. Wise and learned people, tribal leaders, and even priests busied themselves trying to decode dreams and give them weight, significance, and relevance to people's lives. Some saw dreams as a unique platform for communicating with the dead. Others saw dreams as a bridge to spiritual worlds. Tribes united around charismatic dreamers, and many religions and faiths were built upon dreams.

Our historical journey begins more than 2,500 years ago. The most ancient historical finding we have regarding dreams is in the royal library of Ashurbanipal (669-631 BCE), the last queen of the Assyrian empire. During excavations at Nineveh, the capital of Assyria (the Quyunjik Tel, in present-day Iraq), the British archaeologist Sir Austen Henry Layard and his team discovered a real treasure. A chronological library of royal writings was discovered, with religious and mythological texts, contracts, royal grants and regulations, royal missives, a third of Hammurabi's laws, and a variety of administrative documents.

In addition, books and records of various dreams were found there, including the personal dream book of the Assyrian king, which was used by Artemidorus, who lived in the second century CE, in writing the book *Oneirocritica* (*Interpretation of Dreams*). This book divides dreams into those that have a clear message, and those in which symbols appear that require interpretation In a certain sense, Artemidorus created the comparison that the world of psychology would come to understand some 2,000 years later.

But these ancient findings can teach us more than history. According to the anthropologists Edward Tylor and James Frazer, written dreams offer not only a symbol and a historical echo of what was happening in the past, but also portray the development of religious thinking over the years regarding the existence of the Divine and its connection to human beings. The dream records and the descriptions of the Divine can teach us how many believers imagined God for thousands of years. In sharing their dreams, the dreamers also discovered that they shared ways in which God was revealed, and this sharing worked both ways: it enhanced people's concept of God, and it brought about more and more frequent revelations of God through dreams.

Despite the similarities among dreams and dreamers, history shows parallel axes of ancient dreams and cultures in which dreams took on additional dimensions. To understand our own dreams better, we will need to wander back in time, towards ancient cultures that chose to dream and look at dreams differently than the way we do today. Who can say who is right when it comes to dreams?

DREAMS IN NATIVE AMERICAN CULTURES

In Eastern cultures in general, and specifically among the Native American tribes, people saw dreams as a unique human interface that could be observed with human senses. The human capacity to dream dreams, to see things that do not necessarily exist in reality, was viewed as a sort of bridge between this world and other worlds. The dreamers of highly developed dreams, as well as interpreters of dreams everywhere, were accorded great power and gained a mystical aura as they used their ability to advise people on various life challenges.

In the dream space, there is no limit on the spiritual figures that one can dream about. Without restrictions of time and space, and when the boundaries of imagination are breached, everyone has the ability to communicate with gods, spirits, and dead people – and through them – to improve their lives, their experiences, and the way they act. Success in decoding what the future holds earned those dreamers glory and great power in the various Native American tribes.

Here I should note that where power was ascribed to dreams, obedience to dreams was often blind. That is, from the moment dreams were deemed important, the element of randomness of the dream or the dreamer lost most of its weight. Even the most ordinary dream – meaningless and without a solution – was considered important. In ancient initiation rites, the young person, before becoming a man in the tribe, was required to face several challenges. Beyond the physical challenges, taking the form of survival and fighting wild beasts, the young men were required to recount spiritual challenges such as a significant vision or dream. Although we may be more comfortable thinking of this as something distant and ancient, many of the mystical elements of dreams are still found in various forms, as you will see in the coming chapters.

DREAMCATCHERS, BOTH HUMAN AND MATERIAL

If dreams are a bridge, offering free passage between the spirit world and this one, they must be supervised and controlled. Therefore, in tribal cultures such as those of the Native Americans, people served in official positions as "dreamcatchers," with the goal of filtering out bad dreams or saving the dreamer from nightmares. Besides a human guard, whom everyone wanted close by in certain circumstances, people also began to develop means of protection and tools to deal with dreams.

A well-known phenomenon has come to us from the Ojibwa people, later adopted by many other peoples through marriage ties and trade relations with the Ojibwa. As with any good thing, here, too, the story begins with an ancient legend, in this case about the source of the dreamcatcher. According to the legend, a "spider woman" named Asibikaashi cared for children and adults on Earth. When the Ojibwa people spread out to all corners of America, Asibikaashi had difficulty getting to the children, and so the mothers and grandmothers spun magic spider webs for the children from rings of willow wood and sinews or threads from plants. The dreamcatchers filtered out bad dreams and allowed only good thoughts to enter the mind. When the sun rose, the bad dreams would simply disappear. Here the ancient legend ends.

According to tradition, the Ojibwa construct dreamcatchers by knotting sinews in webs around a teardrop-shaped frame or circular hoop, similar to the way that snowshoes are woven. The dreamcatcher is hung above the bed and serves as a talisman and spiritual guard to protect sleeping people – usually children – who are naturally vulnerable to nightmares and bad dreams. The Ojibwa believe that the dreamcatcher affects a person's dreams so that only good dreams are permitted to pass through the filter, while bad dreams remain stuck there.

How does this happen in practice? Here is a short description of the structure of the dreamcatcher: The feathers connected below the ring serve as ladders to absorb good dreams, and the beads on the bottom of the dreamcatcher are tied to various traditional stories. Some tribes identify the knots with the spider, which catches and filters out bad dreams, while others maintain that the good dreams are caught and held by the spider's web. Usually there are 13 points on the web, symbolizing the 13 phases of the moon, but sometimes there are fewer points: 8 points refer to the spider woman; 7 points are connected with the seven prophecies; 6 refer to an eagle; and 5 represent a star. The ring of the dreamcatcher represents the sun and the circle is identified with life.

When a feather falls from the dreamcatcher, the bad dreams disappear. This ensures that the good dreams will come true. By hanging the dreamcatcher over the bed, its purpose is fulfilled; it protects the sleeping person and brings them good dreams. Feathers are also a symbol of love and maternal protection.

The Native Americans are not alone. In Papua New Guinea, there are almost 800 tribes that have been preserved since ancient times. Up until the twentieth century, the tribes continued their cultures and customs, with some still practicing cannibalism. Studies of the Macao people, who agreed to be exposed to modern researchers, revealed how much significance and honor these tribes accorded to dreams. They saw dreams as an opportunity to look into a person's liberated soul, as well as access to a kingdom of knowledge and power. Discussions and the recounting of dreams

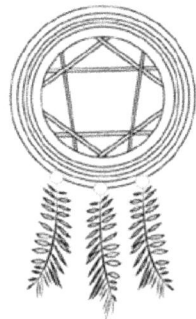

take place even today among various tribes around their campfires, with the tellers anticipating the dreams' realization or asking for help in interpreting them. Without a doubt, some of those tribal ceremonies can also be seen around our own children's campfires.

PYRAMIDS OF DREAMS

Ancient Egyptians also saw dreams as bearing signs and messages from the gods, and various dreams were preserved. One of the most ancient dream books, which for lack of an official title is simply called "The Book of Dreams," is dated to 1300 BCE. This book shows how interpretations of a dream, and the symbols in it, were precisely indicated while raising over 200 interpretations for decoding those heavenly signs. Not everyone's dreams were recorded – only those of the most distinguished and respected members of society, who had the luxury of waking up every morning and taking time to document their dreams, or of people who could share their dreams without fearing that an incorrect interpretation could cause people to look at them suspiciously.

Ancient records of dreams can be found in Sumerian sources, such as *Gudea's Dream*, in Egyptian sources such as *Merneptah's Dream*, and even in ancient Japan. In the famous chronicles of Josephus Flavius, Josephus describes the dream of Jaddua the Priest on the eve of Alexander the Great's arrival in Jerusalem, when God appeared to him and instructed him to adorn himself for the King's arrival. Thus dreams are woven deeply into the culture and history of the East, the Native Americans, and the ancient Egyptians. The desire to preserve and document dreams appears not only in famous people's diaries, but also in the increasing popularity of the dreamcatchers, as one can see by the many Internet sites selling them. Could our dreams be influenced by the fact that most of those dreamcatchers are produced in third-world countries? It seems that we will never know the answer to that question.

DREAMS IN ANCIENT GREECE

What about Ancient Greece? The country that gave us so much philosophy also brought a unique approach to dreams. Homer, the greatest poet of Ancient Greece, lived in the eighth century BCE; his *The Odyssey* includes descriptions and rhymes relating to dreams. The 19th book, in which Odysseus converses with Penelope while his feet are being washed, refers to dreams:[2]

> *There are two gates that open for shadowy dreams:*
> *one is made of horn, the other of ivory.*
> *Dreams that come through the gate of carved ivory*
> *deceive us with promises that are unfulfilled.*
> *But those that come through the gate of gleaming horn*
> *tell the dreamer of what will come to pass.*

Homer describes the belief, widely held at the time, that true dreams come through the "horn gate" as opposed to false dreams that come through the "ivory gate." A similar parallel appears in the Babylonian Talmud (Tractate Berachot 55), which states, "True dreams come via an angel and false dreams come via a demon."

Another famous Greek, whom you've surely heard about (and if not, this is a great opportunity to get acquainted with him) is Hippocrates, who saw dreams as a kind of reflection of the soul and even took upon himself the role of dream interpreter. Hippocrates, born in 460 BCE, achieved great honor during his lifetime, and even more after his death, when he was memorialized by a multitude of

---

2   English translation taken from: https:// PITBR/Greek/Odyssey19.php#anchor_Toc90268708

legends about medical miracles that he had wrought; beneficiaries of his miraculous cures included Athenians during the plague, and King Perdiccas I of Macedon, among others. Hippocrates laid the foundations of medical ethics and is primarily remembered for the Hippocratic Oath, still taken by physicians at their swearing-in ceremonies.

Claudius Galen, an early Greek physician who was court physician to the Roman emperor Marcus Aurelius, exalted dreams and their role. Galen's name is remembered to this day by a pharmaceutical formulation protocol called the "Galenic Formulation." Maimonides later referred to Galen in one of his epistles, taking issue with his outlook, but at the same time admiring his wealth of scientific knowledge and his great medical wisdom. Galen noted that many life-saving drugs were revealed to him in dreams. He conducted applied research on dreams, requiring every patient to describe not only their symptoms but also their dreams.

In the ancient world, one accepted method for receiving a dream was "incubation" – a technique for obtaining information from a dream by sleeping in a sacred place along with performing ritual acts. Many researchers have dealt with this phenomenon, including Cox-Miller, Flannery, Louis, Dodds and others. By inviting the higher powers, the dreamer would bring about a dream theophany, or a visible manifestation of a deity. Dr. Haim Weiss, in his article "Incubation Dreams and Inviting Dreams in the Ancient World," notes that there is no evidence in Rabbinic literature of Jews using sleep rituals at temples or sacred places, in contrast to Christianity, in which sleeping in churches was highly encouraged in order to attain revelation from some saint or another.

An example of one sleep ritual is the temple at Epidaurus to the god Asclepius, who is mentioned in the Hippocratic Oath as the one in whose name one takes the oath. Asclepius was the Greek and Roman god of medicine and dreams. The Asclepieion in the Epidaurus shrine was thought to be the most important healing center in the ancient world. It was defined as a place of the healing gods; to find the precise medicine for their illness, sick people would spend the night in the *enkoimeteria* (a sleeping hall with 160 places) and wait for an "incubation of the dream." During their stay in the temple, guests were invited to partake of potions and herbal mixtures that would cause them to fall into a deep sleep, and the resulting dream they dreamed there received further validity. During the night, Asclepius would appear to them and reveal the precise medicine for their illness. Archeological excavations at the site have uncovered clay forms in the shape of human body parts, as well as wall inscriptions testifying to the great honor accorded to that temple and the healing capacity of dreams.

Now we have seen that Greece was not only a place where philosophy flourished, but also a place that opened a window to dreamers and dreams. Have the sleep temples disappeared entirely? Don't sleep labs, as well as modern dream workshops, echo ancient Greece? We'll see that more than a few Greek theories prevail among humankind even today, 2,000 years later.

DREAMS IN THE ORIENT AND IN BUDDHISM

The mystique surrounding dreams is well suited to the Orient, and the history of Oriental peoples shows that mysticism and the soul are bound up in their cultures. Chinese scholars believed that dreams occur when the spirit, the *hun*, temporarily separates from the body and can commune with the spirits, with dead souls, or with the gods. In the fourteenth century CE, all visitors to an important city were required to spend the first night in the temple of that city's god, so that they could receive the messages – a custom that echoes the incubation temples of the Classical Period.

The Oriental scholar A. Leo Oppenheim, in his book *The Interpretation of Dreams in the Ancient Near East*, surveyed ancient dream interpretation in that part of the world, while at the same time showing how distinctively Oriental concepts permeated American culture and became part of the consensus. According to the Buddhist view, it is possible to reach enlightenment via dreams, particularly in a state of daydreaming.

In contrast to the widespread view, which demands control and hyper-responsiveness, Buddhism ascribes importance to passivity and allowing feelings and thoughts to surface. Thus, as in a dream, when the dreamer is detached from perception of space and time, in waking dreaming the daydreamer should actually feel alert through hearing the sounds and sensations that are normally silenced in daily life. Many Buddhists perform techniques of quieting and intention in order to improve the character of the dream and allow the dreamer's mind and body to be influenced by the calm with which the dreamer enters the dream.

Later, in the modern era, meditations took the form of the mindfulness method, in which the practitioner seeks to turn his attention to experiences and phenomena taking place at that moment, but without the judgment that characterizes wakefulness. In the digital age, with its many stimuli, practicing mindfulness can help calm the stress and tension that many people experience. This method has four main components: beginner's mind, which is openness and curiosity about phenomena as they are, like a child who sees something for the first time; aware attention; presence and attentiveness to the totality of present processes, moment by moment; and non-judgmental acceptance.

In our digital world, where we are led to endless pursuit, the Orient offers a break from this frenzy, as well as a calm that often becomes a dream for many seeking serenity. Daydreams, like sleeping dreams, allow us to disconnect and step back to observe ourselves and what we are going through.

MUHAMMAD'S DREAM AND THE WORLD OF ISLAM

Not only history and culture arose around dreams; monotheistic religions have also accorded dreams a place of honor. In addition to Judaism, to which I have dedicated a separate chapter, the Islamic religion should be noted in this context. It was founded by Muhammad ben Abdallah and is currently the religion of 1.8 billion people, a quarter of the world's population. According to Islamic tradition, the Prophet Muhammad, founder of Islam and the last of the prophets, was born in Mecca in 571 CE and in his youth dreamed terrible dreams that caused a neurological disease and insanity. Seeking a cure for his soul, he met Waraqah, his wife's uncle, who had tried Christianity and Judaism and chosen to follow a different path. As a result of this encounter, Muhammad studied the way of life of the Christians from the land of Kush and the Jews in Mecca, until he abandoned the idea of the Holy Trinity and chose a monotheistic faith. At the age of 40, Muhammad encountered the Angel Gabriel for the first time in the Cave of Hira on Jabal al-Nour. Muhammad chose to tell his wife about the encounter, fearing that it was an evil spirit that had taken hold of him, and tried to end his life. Three years later, Muhammad again encountered Gabriel and asked him to cover him with a blanket until he heard a voice saying to him, "O you, enveloped in a mantle, stand up and warn, and pronounce the greatness of your Lord, and purify your clothes, and keep away from filth..." (Koran, 74:1-5). After some time, a trader named Abu Bakr decided to join Muhammad, eventually becoming "the first Caliph and the Pillar of Islam," and after him, the young Uthman, who married one of Muhammad's daughters and became the third

Caliph, and Bilal, the freed slave, who was the first *muezzin* to call the worshipers to the mosque.

The Quraysh, a tribe of merchants operating in the Arabian Peninsula, to which the Prophet Muhammad belonged, despised Muhammad and the new movement he had chosen to create. Their mocking insults included, "Madman, man of spirit, dreamer of dreams, erring and causing others to err, or writer of poetry,"[3] Quraysh members tried to kill Muhammad, and after many plots against him, Muhammad hid together with Abu Bakr in a cave. On the 16th day of the sixth month in 622, they fled to Yathrib, the "El-Medina." The year 622, the year of Muhammad's migration (*hejira*), is the beginning of the Islamic calendar, which shows the importance of Muhammad's new place of residence and the honor he received there. It is interesting to note that even in the new location, Muhammad tried to win the Jews' hearts; in the beginning, he even commanded his followers to fast on Yom Kippur, to pray facing Jerusalem, and to believe in the coming of the Messiah. After the Jews mocked his dreams and his words, however, he commanded his followers to fast during the month of Ramadan and not on Yom Kippur, to pray facing Mecca, and to persecute the Jews with sharp language.

The Islamic call to prayer, the *Adhan*, also originated in the dream of one of Muhammad's companions. Dreams in Islam are accorded significance not only in Muhammad's actions but also in Biblical scenes that appear in the Koran. The Binding of Isaac is described in the Koran in Chapter 37 as a dialogue that takes place in a dream. In this version, Abraham reveals to Isaac that he saw in a dream that he must sacrifice him and asks to hear his son's opinion. According to the Koran, Isaac answers that his father Abraham must do as he was told in the dream.

3   https://www.daat.ac.il/encyclopedia/value.asp?id1=970

The Islamic world has always had a fascination with everything connected to dreams. The most famous figure in this regard is Halil ben Shahin al Zairi, author of *Advice and Hints about Knowledge of the Meaning of Dreams*.[4] Al Zairi's book served as a sort of *Guide for the Perplexed* for dreamers and those seeking to understand dreams. Ibn Khaldun, another well-known Islamic writer, classified dreams as a type of science belonging to the "science of dream interpretation." In their writings and autobiographical journals, Islamic sages did not hesitate to weave in dreams of encounters with God and with Muhammad, as well as other heavenly visions. Thus, Muslims continue to dream and to give dreams their unique touch.

THE DREAMS OF LUCREZIA DE LEON AND DREAMS IN SIXTEENTH-CENTURY SPAIN

After we have visited Iraq, Greece, Egypt, Papua New Guinea, and the Orient, we must not leave Western Europe standing idly by. This time we'll take a look at a special story about a distinguished Spanish dreamer named Lucrezia de Leon. Lucrezia was born to a merchant in Madrid in 1567 and, like other women, had a strictly religious upbringing and was destined to serve primarily as a wife and mother. Lucrezia couldn't read and write, but by chance served in the court of the Spanish King Philip II (the 15th king of Spain), known as "El Prudente." From the moment she met the King, Lucrezia began having dreams of a prophetic character, while her father tried to dissuade her from recounting them publicly lest they suffer harm at the hands of the Inquisition.

Gradually, however, Lucrezia began to tell her dreams to anyone willing to pay for the privilege. The Spanish Armada was a military naval force known as the "Great Armada" or the "Invincible Armada." In one campaign, it attempted to invade England and

---

4   Carl Brockelmann, Geschichte der Arabischen Literatur, Supplement, (Leiden: Brill, 1938), 2:166

depose Queen Elizabeth I. Lucrezia dreamed that the Invincible Armada would be beaten and, when her dream was affirmed, she earned local and economic glory and many followers.

The king, however, was enraged by Lucrezia's public attention, coupled with her vision of the Armada's failure, for which he was held responsible, and he ordered the Inquisition to arrest her on charges of heresy and sedition. Throughout her imprisonment and the tortures she suffered, she carefully documented her dreams. To this day, psychologists have seen Lucrezia as someone who chose to use advanced cognitive techniques, and many books have been written around the figure of the young woman who gained exceptional fame in Spain thanks to her dreams.

DREAMS IN THE PATTERNS OF HISTORY AND IN MODERN CULTURE

Dreams, as you must have noticed, have accompanied humanity all along the timeline of history, and researchers concur with this popular perception. Thus, for example, the psychiatrist Anthony Stevens, in his 1995 *Private Myths*, divides the view of dreams throughout history into three categories: cultures that believe that dreams are messages from supernatural forces, those who believe that dreams are actual experiences due to the soul's "external wanderings" during sleep, and those that adopt the naturalistic approach that dreams are a natural result of normal psychological processes. It is possible, of course, for a culture to believe in several of these theories at the same time. Through the lens of history we see dreams divided into categories that show how dreams developed and how they developed the dreamers.

Also in 1995, Robert L. Van de Castle published a book called *Our Dreaming Mind*, in which he showed how history is filled with dreams, beginning with the dreams of ancient Sumerian kings and up until the dream research of nineteenth-century psychologists. It would not be an exaggeration to say that dreams have preserved history as much as history has preserved dreams. Dreams and dreamers have made things happen and made daring choices, yet dreams have always been shrouded in a veil of ambiguity and mystery, despite their impact on all of our lives. The psychologist Rubin Naiman claims that the lack of importance that modern society ascribes to dreams could be destructive to everyone's mental health.

Dreams were not just the province of far-out therapists and weirdos, but also many famous figures in history. More precisely, not so long ago there lived an American who, besides being a great dreamer, served as the sixth president of the United States: John Quincy Adams. Adams was not only a great statesman, but an avid writer and used to keep personal diaries about the events he experienced. In fact, in 1779 Adams began keeping a diary and did not stop until his death in 1848. This diary, occupying 50 volumes, offers a glimpse into history as well as accounts of the dreams that he chose to record.

Records of dreams were not only found in the diaries of famous people. Various newspapers published readers' dreams and the famous newspaper *New York World* ran a competition for the "Champion of Dreams." Other dreams were not publicized but were documented, such as dreams recorded by British officers while they were being held prisoner by the Nazis from 1940-1942. This is similar to another dream documentation, that of Major Kent Hopkins, who, had it not been for pneumonia, would have been able to publish his doctoral thesis documenting research he conducted, including meticulous daily dream records of 79 prisoners held at Laufen Castle in Bavaria. At the beginning of the twentieth century, in his renowned book, *10,000 Dreams Interpreted*, Gustavus Hindman Miller collected no less than 10,000 examples of dreams and put them into a sort of "dream dictionary," in which he interpreted and sorted types of dreams and the symbols appearing in them. A century later, in 2011, Linda Shields proposed an amended version of the dictionary containing 12,000 dreams, noting that she believed that 2,000 more entries should be added (beyond the corrections and additions). This is due to technological advances and the appearance of objects that were unknown in Miller's time, such as cellular phones, computers, televisions, etc. In the current era, documentations of dreams are published constantly on various blogs and internet sites.

Modern researchers both touched on and avoided dreams until they managed to assemble the puzzle pieces and create a new field of dream research. From the moment it reached the medical clinic, it immediately gained a place of honor in both popular culture and intellectual circles. In 1892 Charles Child of Wesleyan University began to speak about dreams in academia, inviting students to share their dreams and taking the dreams seriously. Child asked the students if they had solved a problem in their dream; a third of them reported solutions achieved via a dream. Eighty years later, sleep researcher William Dement of Stanford University even asked his students to go to sleep with an unsolved problem, but the data he obtained were not significant: only 7 out of 500 students reported that they had achieved a solution.

Dreams themselves, therefore, have undergone a sort of transformation throughout history and human culture, and the dreamers, who once were clad in leaves around campfires in remote forest clearings, began to appear in laboratories, surrounded by lab coats and various MRI machines.

DEATHBED DREAMS

It is impossible to talk about history and culture without mentioning death. Death has always accompanied humanity and preoccupied it, so it is only logical that various cultures throughout human history would ascribe great significance to the dreams that a dying person describes just before death. The dreams would often identify the coming of the end of the world, oftentimes emphasizing specific ideas or information that the dying person sought to convey to those around him before his death. In the Babylonian Talmud, sleep is described as one-sixtieth of death; that is, every day the living encounter a certain point of contact with death.

It is interesting to note that in Greek mythology, the god of sleep, Hypnos, and the god of death, Thanatos, are twin brothers. According to the Greek poet Hesiodos, in the eighth century BCE, the two brothers have a third brother, who is the god of dreams. Thus a sort of family relationship was created between death, sleep, and dreams. Dreams also appear in the story of Agamemnon, another figure from Greek mythology who was the great-grand-son of Tantalus and the child of Atreus and Aerope. Agamemnon dreams about Nestor, a decorated warrior in the Greek army, as someone who accompanies Agamemnon during both his dreams and his waking hours.

THE DREAM INDUSTRY IN CULTURE AND IN THE FUTURE

Dreams have not ceased to bear great significance in people's lives. Dreams appear in various forms and permeate the movie industry, television programs, books, plays, and people's entire cultural environment. Dreams are one human experience that has remained dim and hidden despite all the technological advances. The veil of mystery is what makes people not only share their dreams on social media and write about them, but also turn them into merchandise. Many seek to cling to a future or apocalyptic dream, or a dialogue with people who have died, as a meaningful sign. Nowadays the dreams of dying people are documented in a number of sites on the internet and found on Amazon, apparently in an attempt to corroborate what they said against what happens in the future. In addition, today there is an industry seeking to publicize the dreams of people dealing with various syndromes, such as different types of autism. Think of it this way: a lot has changed in the last 1,000 years. Language, thinking, culture, food, clothing, manners . . . what hasn't changed? But there is one thing that has managed to remain the same, that keeps raising more question marks tan exclamation points: dreams. Such a psychological complex calls for psychotherapy.

History and culture are intertwined; together they teach us how much weight and significance has been given to dreams over time, and how the concept of dreams changed from culture to culture. Up until now we have taken a broad look at cultures and at history, allowing us a bird's-eye view of humanity. But humanity is composed of many individuals, and each individual is a world of his own. Accordingly, dreams themselves must be investigated and treated appropriately, with every treatment beginning on the psychologist's couch.

2

DREAMS ON THE PSYCHOLOGIST'S COUCH

A COUCH OR AN ARMCHAIR?

Many of us have encountered or currently encounter the psychologist's couch. It is difficult to say exactly when, but it seems to have become a consensus that, like a car, our psyches need a comprehensive tune-up from time to time. If we are already on the topic of the psyche, dreams can offer a way in to what we carry within us. What are dreams? Are they mere nonsense, or do they perhaps contain symbols that merit our attention in our daily lives? It would not be an exaggeration to say that philosophers and psychologists are struggling to break through the mystery surrounding dreams. If in the previous chapter we looked at humanity from a distance, now we will enter our consciousness and our brains. Like any series of psychological therapy sessions, we will begin by getting to know dreams and we will pass on the baton of research to the world of psychology

DREAMS AS A NECESSARY CONDITION FOR SURVIVAL AND SUCCESS

Today it is impossible to discuss modern dream research without mentioning Alice Robb. Robb is not a psychologist or a researcher, but rather a journalist who writes about science in the U.S. Her lack of an official position actually allowed her to write a unique book in 2017 called *Why We Dream*. In this book, Robb broke new ground by discussing current research and dreams, alongside experiments she conducted on herself regarding lucid dreaming and dreams' influence on her life. In the sixth chapter of her book, Robb deals with dreams as preparation for life, and she mentions two significant anecdotes: a theory and experiment that forge a new path in using dreams not only as a model for rummaging through our past, but also as something that can help lead us to a rosier future.

1. **The dream as strengthening**. In 2000, the "Threat Simulation Theory" (TST) was published by several researchers, including the Finnish researchers Raija-Leena Punamaki and Annti Revonsuo. Within the framework of this theory, one can show how dreams serve us as a sort of psychologist, with no need to pay or come to a specific place to receive treatment. Every night we unload experiences and prolonged anxieties and allow dreams to give them expression. Our dialogue via the dream not only unloads but also strengthens us and improves our chances of survival after we manage to "cleanse ourselves" of the negative feelings that permeate a large portion of our dreams.

2. **The dream as a component of survival.** In 2004, an experiment was conducted that proved dreams' connection to survival. Researchers deprived rats of REM (Rapid Eye Movement) sleep – which we will discuss later – and allowed them only "normal" sleep without dreams. After a few days they compared these rats with those who dreamed dreams, looking at how they handled threatening situations and their attempts to survive a threat during the experiment. The group of rats that did not dream erred in decision-making and failed to act decisively in situations in which they could be saved. Even when those rats received stimulants that were intended to make them alert, they did not survive.

It turns out that not only animals' survival is enhanced through dreams. Studies on medical students over the years discovered that the students who dreamed about a test before they took it – mainly those who had bad dreams about the test – actually did better. That is, the dream was a sort of initial encounter with the test and the fears connected to it, and thus in reality they were in an environment that they had already gotten used to in some way. The dream not only enabled survival behavior, but improved success.

Dreams, as we noted in the chapter on their history, have been viewed as heavenly signs, a substitute for prophecy, or communication with spirits. What all these theories and concepts have in common is the view that the dream is *external* to the person – i.e., the dream's interface with the person is on the outside and not the inside. The first to change this concept or, more accurately, the most outstanding figure in history who changed the entire direction of thought regarding dreams – directing them inwards – was Sigmund

Freud. Today it is impossible to discuss psychology without taking into account the unique Dr. Freud (1856-1939), the psychologist and neurologist who was the father of psychoanalytic treatment, which leaves significant room for the patient himself, making him an active participant in his treatment and its success.

DREAMS IN FREUD'S THEORY

In the fields of psychoanalysis and psychotherapy, Freud ascribed significance and status to dreams. He is considered to be one of the pioneers of the concept that a dream is a significant psychological activity. As such, he saw dreams as a tool for psychological processing, serving as a lifeline for the psyche to express itself and process thoughts, both conscious and subconscious, with which a person interfaces during his lifetime. For Freud, the contents of a dream belonged not only to the past or to unloading, but were also something that required attention and treatment in the present, in order to help the body and psyche process the challenges facing a person, as well as formulate plans for the future. This aspect is somewhat reminiscent of the modern-day studies we mentioned above regarding the importance of dreams to our day-to-day survival

On July 24, 1895, Freud dreamed his famous "Irma's Injection dream, which he discussed in his book *The Interpretation of Dreams*. The book was ultimately reprinted many times, despite the fact that the first edition did not sell out for eight years. In later editions, Freud incorporated his insights regarding psychoanalysis. His dream research continued for 39 more years, during which he further developed his concept of dreams. Another book, *On Dreams*, came out a year after *The Interpretation of Dreams*. In it, Freud challenged the accepted assumption of his time, according to which the source of dreams was "outside" – that is, from some external source – and that one could attain knowledge about the world via dreams. Freud presented his conjecture that the source of the dream was the dreamer himself, and thus dreams express internal events according to certain rules. To understand these rules, the various elements comprising a dream must be broken down into their components.

Via dreams, Freud unveiled a theory on the internal mechanisms of the body and mind. The dream enables the dreamer to express what is going on in his heart, consciously and subconsciously, without limits, bringing a synergistic flood of the shifting defense mechanisms that comprise fear. Thus, in parallel, the release in a dream allows strengthening of the body through high-quality sleep. Freud came to the insight that people have information unavailable to conscious awareness by studying the results of hypnosis experiments by the French neurologist Hippolyte Bernheim. Bernheim discovered that his patients did not remember anything right after coming out of the hypnotic state, but after questioning and investigation, it was found that the memories created during hypnosis indeed existed.

Freud distinguished between a dream's revealed content and hidden content; the latter could be decoded via a thorough analysis of the dream and its various associations. A dream's hidden content (which includes erotic and sexual content, according to Freud) is not necessarily known, and is mediated through censorship that we perform during our waking hours. The work of dream analysis is done in four stages:

1. **Condensation.** Presenting many hypotheses regarding an element revealed in a dream.

2. **Displacement.** Replacing an element in the dream with something that was not explicitly shown in the dream.

3. **Symbolism.** Taking thoughts expressed in words by the dreamer and turning them into visual images. Transition from words to image.

4. **Secondary revision.** Integrating the images from the dream analysis to create a unified, continuous narrative for the dream.

Dream interpretation uses symbols to neutralize the censoring mechanism and allow one to identify the components and unpack their associations. Today, Freud's method of dream interpretation is a central pillar of various psychoanalytic practices. If you start telling your psychologist about your dreams, you will most likely be able to identify Freud's stages between the lines.

IRMA'S INJECTION

Freud's famous dream was meticulously recorded and analyzed down to its most minute details – for 17 pages – to enable it to be studied. This dream was mentioned as one that Freud managed to experience fully, and to which he ascribed great significance. Before recounting the dream, Freud explained the relevant circumstances, including a meeting with a patient who was not progressing due to disagreements between him and her about the recommended treatment. Freud's friend Otto told him that he had met the patient at a resort and noted that her health had not fully improved. Freud felt that Otto's narrative reflected dissatisfaction with the treatment on the part of Irma's family. Later, on the night between July 23 and 24, 1895, Freud dreamed the following:

A large hall – numerous guests, whom we were receiving. Among them was Irma. I at once took her to one side, as though to answer her letter and to reproach her for not having accepted my "solution" yet. I said to her: "If you still get pains, it's really only your fault." She replies: "If you only knew what pains I've got now in my throat and stomach and abdomen— it's choking me."

I was alarmed and looked at her. She looked pale and puffy. I thought to myself that after all I must be missing some organic trouble. I took her to the window and looked down her throat, and she showed signs of recalcitrance, like women with artificial dentures. I thought to myself that there was really no need for her to do that...

She then opened her mouth properly and, on the right, I found a big white patch; at another place I saw extensive whitish grey scabs upon some remarkable curly structures which were evidently modelled on the turbinal bones of the nose. I at once called in Dr. M., and he repeated the examination and confirmed it ...

Dr. M. looked quite different from usual; he was very pale, he walked with a limp and his chin was clean-shaven ... My friend Otto was now standing beside her as well, and my friend Leopold was percussing her through her bodice and saying: 'She has a dull area low down on the left.' He also indicated that a portion of the skin on her left shoulder was infiltrated. (I noticed this, just as he did, in spite of her dress.) ...

Dr. M. said: 'There's no doubt it's an infection, but no matter; dysentery will supervene and the toxin will be eliminated. We were directly aware, too, of the origin of the infection. Not long before, when she was feeling unwell, my friend Otto had given her an injection of a preparation of propyl, propyls ... propionic acid ... trimethylamin (and I saw before me the formula for this printed in heavy type) Injections of this sort ought not to be given so thoughtlessly ... And probably the syringe had not been clean... [5]

Freud assumes that the ability to interpret dreams lies with professionals, while a layman has only limited ability to interpret his own dreams, even if he is Freud himself. The therapist, in contrast to the dreamer, prepares himself, and it is in fact his external position that enables him to identify the symbols and censoring mechanisms of which the dreamer himself is unaware. Later, Freud's followers were divided on the manner of treatment and "dream work," with each one defining their own general rules, including categories of thinking whose classification and definition are the keys to deciphering a dream. If you sit on the psychologist's couch, most likely you will encounter some constellation of Freud's ideas in the person sitting opposite you. Don't forget where you met him first.

DREAMS IN JUNG'S THEORY

Carl Gustav Jung was a psychiatrist and psychoanalyst, one of Freud's senior students and his designated heir. Jung started out studying exact sciences, but he could not resist trying to understand the intricacies of the psyche in general, and his own in particular. For this reason, he transferred his focus to psychology. In 1912

5   Sigmund Freud (1900). *The Interpretation of Dreams*

Jung published *The Psychology of the Unconscious.* In the book, Jung took issue with Freud's view, which hastened the parting of ways between the opinionated and ambitious teacher and the student. Jung left his mark not only in the extensive literature and concepts he introduced, and his famous students, Erich Neumann and Julius Spier, but also in the famous MBTI method (Myers-Briggs Type Indicator), a personality evaluation method based on Jung's ideas. By the way, the disagreement between Freud and Jung still continues between their respective students, so one could say that it has yet to be resolved.

Jung's interpretation of dreams, not surprisingly, differed from Freud's. He took issue with Freud's melding of the subconscious and the conscious and viewing them as a single entity, holding this to be wrong both as a psychological method and as a means of understanding dreams. He held that the conscious and subconscious should be viewed as layers, and that underneath the layers of the conscious and sub-consciousness is the layer of the "collective unconscious" that is shared by all humanity. This layer contains both chaos and primitivism on the one hand, and creativity, wealth, and uniqueness on the other. The only chance we have to glimpse all these is via dreams. While Freud chose to focus the unconscious on erotic drives connected to sexuality and various perversions, Jung found in the unconscious layer a universal symbolic language that should be listened to attentively via dreams.

In the world of the unconscious, Jung identified archetypes that have been preserved and taken root in humanity's collective memory. Jung described the archetype as a channel through which living water flowed for centuries, carving out a path for itself. The longer the water has been flowing through it, the more likely it is that the water will flow through it again – sooner or later. About archetypes, Jung said that the language of symbols is the natural language of the psyche, and from here the close proximity between art and psychology. Without recognizing archetypes, which are a kind of cultural heritage embedded in the depths of each individual's unconscious, it is impossible to understand the various layers of each person's internal world.

Among Jung's archetypes, one can identify the "ego" (connected to identity and adaptation); the "shadow"(the dark side of a person's personality); the "persona" (the image that the person chooses to market himself to society, which contains a certain falsity); the "anima" (femininity) and the "animus" (masculinity) (in his approach, each sex has a measure of masculinity and femininity in different proportions); and the "self-mandala" (striving for wholeness). There are other archetypes in a person: the father figure (which can symbolize elevated divinity or sexual lust in the image of the Devil); the mother figure (the child's positive and negative images regarding his real mother); the wise elder (intelligence and knowledge as well as other insights); and other archetypes such as Mother Earth, animals, etc.

To conceptualize the realm of the unconscious, Jung suggested calling it "collective man." This is an image of a person that combines the characteristics of both sexes, beyond youth, age, birth, and death, and holds millions of years of experience, making the universal subconscious "almost immortal." Despite humans' unceasing quest for the distinctions between various groups living all across the globe, there is no doubt that this description is an attempt to formulate universal characteristics for humanity.

If so, according to Jung, all the archetypes create those "great dreams" that transmit a message to the dreamer, as in one giant show, even when it seems to him to be a dream from afar. The great dreams are universal, shared by all humanity despite differences in religion, race, sex, and location along the axis of history. In contrast, small dreams are subjective and interface with daily experiences. One way or another, a dream is a small door behind which the deepest, most intimate psychological depths are hidden, depths that cannot be reached except via the dream. This is indeed a door that is worth trying to open.

It turns out that dreams are part of a person's development and self-fulfillment, processes described by Jung's term "individuation." Here, too, Jung disagreed with Freud: Freud viewed a person's early years as the main force shaping their personality, while Jung saw the construction of the personality (and the psyche) as a gradual process taking place throughout the person's life, during which skills and tools to achieve his goals are acquired. This construction process, according to Jung, takes up to half of someone's life, ending mostly around the 40s (an age defined in Judaism as the "age of wisdom" and an age that permits a person to study hidden aspects of Judaism according to some Ashkenazi approaches). After this age, a person begins to become acquainted with all the internal sides he has developed, and tries to balance them.

REINFORCING THE PSYCHOLOGICAL APPROACH – ON EXTERNAL STIMULI AND THEIR EFFECTS ON DREAMS

Did it ever happen that you felt like you were falling out of bed, and right away, instinctively, you thrust out an arm or a leg? Apparently, you are not alone. This phenomenon is connected to the same psychological approach that ascribes dreams to what is going on within the person and not to some higher worlds. This approach was further reinforced by one of the most outstanding figures in dream research, who has become somewhat anonymous over the years: the nineteenth-century physician Louis Alfred Maury, who was one of the first to delve into the research of dreams. Since this wasn't a widely accepted choice in those days, Maury had to conduct his experiments on himself as he investigated whether changes in his external environment affected his dreams. On finding that his dreams changed according to actions conducted by his assistants while he slept, Maury arrived at a far-reaching conclusion: The source of dreams lay in the person himself, with no connection to any spiritual mysticism.

The experiments he conducted on himself were not the only thing leading Maury to his radical conclusions. In 1861 he began to wonder about the essence of dreams and what took place in them, and published an article on sleep and dreams. In the article, he pondered whether one could point to a connection between a dream and an external stimulus (in the same period, these ideas also appeared in dream descriptions of the psychologist Henry Havelock-Ellis (1859-1939)). Would a person who was sprinkled with water or tickled during sleep react in his dream, via the subconscious, similarly to the way he would react if awake? Or was the dream entirely unconnected to the reaction in reality? Maury also laid the foundations for studying the connection between different types of dreams and the stage at which they appear during sleep. Thus, Maury asked whether dreams became more realistic and significant in deeper stages of sleep, whether there is a connection between dreams and age and, primarily, how important a person's dreams are.

Maury left his mark on a significant part of the world's population as his proposed approach eventually became widely known. He suggested that even though we experience many varied events during a dream, the dream itself is significantly shorter than the dreamer's experience of it. Many events are compressed into a dream, but it lasts only a tiny fraction of the time it takes for the person to imagine all those events. Maury's theory was based on his famous "guillotine dream," during which a series of events led up to his being taken out for execution by guillotine. When he awoke, he discovered that his bed frame had fallen on his neck while he was dreaming, and this is what caused him to conclude that all the events in the dream were compressed into the time between this event and the time he was awakened by the pain.

This is an excellent opportunity to mention the inclusive approach of the French philosopher Henri Bergson (1859-1941), who explained that the truth lies somewhere in the middle, and that dreams have both aspects: They are indeed memories and things that surface from the subconscious, but how they surface and take shape is connected to an external, physical stimulus. Bergson put the cart before the horse, as we will see later regarding the dynamic between the inner and outer realms.

PSYCHIATRY, DREAMS, AND THE SELF

It is impossible to discuss psychology without discussing psychiatry, which is the operational arm of psychology regarding any kind of mental health treatment. Yes, I know that psychologists and psychiatrists want to kill me for this comparison, but if you try taking a step back and looking at it from a distance, perhaps you will agree with me. There are those who have done a wonderful job of combining the two, one of whom is Heinz Kohut, founder of the Self-psychology movement. Self-psychology relates to the need to find the patient's real self, which is done by prolonged examination of the patient's experience and transferring his suppressed emotional relationship to the therapist.

Kohut advocated a method in which one must touch the

narcissistic melancholy and the disorder in order to understand the patient and achieve the desired therapeutic result. Every person, and particularly those suffering from psychiatric problems that require treatment, has his own self-identity (called the "self") that requires self-appreciation alongside confirmation from his surroundings and the experience of admiring someone who is similar to him. These needs are expressed quite openly during childhood, such as when the boy tries to be like his father, wanting to work in his father's profession, and the girl needs to dress up like her mother.

Applying his method, Kohut discovered something interesting. The dreams of patients who suffered problems related to the self were found to differ from the dreams of "normal" people. Those patients have the types of dreams in which the self-state appears, and the therapist must identify the dreamer's associations and assemble them in order to trace one of the three needs that require treatment and repair via self-psychology. It should be emphasized that according to Kohut, there is no need for interpretation requiring expertise, but rather identification of the thread that weaves those dreams together and attribution of the dreams to one of the three needs of the self. Yes, that means that we, too, can be our own best psychiatrists.

CHARACTERISTICS OF DREAMS

Up until now, we have discussed the general approach to dreams among psychologists. But what about the contents of a dream? Can dreams be characterized and divided into categories?

According to Erich Fromm in his *The Forgotten Language*, the language of dreams is the language of symbols. In this, he echoes the approaches of Freud and Jung, believing like Jung in a sort of universal language, unique and singular, common to all humanity with no distinction of religion, race, or gender, over the course of history. The language of symbols is one of intensity and association, with the contents of the dream being influenced by internal experiences, feelings, and thoughts as though they were experienced in the outer world.

It should be emphasized that the new objects created by technology absolutely affect the contents of dreams, for it is a fact that we dream about technological appliances that did not exist when our parents were our age. Smart phones, drones, online worlds, and even artificial intelligence have all become part of our dreams. But at the same time, the general language of the dream does not change. The unvarying language and the use of symbols, even if the symbols themselves do vary, are in accord with Fromm's approach. The dream does not deal with itself and its goals, but observes an internal world devoid of space and time. This approach is somewhat different from what we have discussed above, but still of supreme importance. At any rate, Erich Fromm, lamenting the fact that dreams get shoved into a corner, asserts that they have features and logical rules by which they can be explained.

One heir to the universalist approach to dreams is the Israeli psychologist Yitzhak Levin. In his book *The Psychology of Dreams*, he sketches lines that characterize the dreams we dream:

1. **Image.** Unlike thinking, a dream is mostly visual, and presents sights that the dreamer observes or appears in. The intellectual thinking that we use in our waking hours is mostly verbal and conceptual. Even in a telepathic dream, which we will discuss below, researchers have found that words cannot be transmitted, but only an image, and it is this image that ultimately enables transmission of the

dream. It should be added that even when some equation appears with its solution, or written sentences, they will appear in the dream as accompanying a certain image and not separately on their own.

2. **Involvement in the dream.** The dreamer sometimes participates significantly in the dream, and at other times is merely an observer. The common denominator between the two is the absence of "awake consciousness" which frees the dreamer from defending or attacking to achieve his goals and objectives, leaving him to merely observe from the side (with one exception that we will discuss later).

3. **Containment.** During the dream, the dreamer does not dispute the events in the dream, even if they are events that go beyond the reality and the environment he knows. The "Don Quixote" phenomenon that we discussed above, in which a person leaves the paralysis of a dream and responds with physical actions, is considered an exception to standard dreams and dreamers.

4. **Passivity.** The dreamer does not take initiative or act in the dream. Note that there is a difference between involvement and awareness and passivity, with the main emphasis on the fact that the dreamer does not initiate the script, but rather allows the dream to unfold on its own. Even when it seems like the dreamer is involved, he does not control his involvement directly (except in the lucid dreaming technique). The level of his involvement and participation varies from dream to dream and is not fixed.

5. **Forgetting.** A person accumulates experiences and memories during his lifetime, some of which leave a significant mark on him. Even if a great deal of time has passed since the encounter, a person can remember his experiences, sometimes with the help of certain aids. In contrast to memory and experiences, most dreams do not leave significant marks on us, and therefore we tend to forget them.

6. **Accompanied by emotions.** Dreams are not just images and a play that the dreamer is observing. Many times a dream arouses emotions and bodily sensations during sleep. The figures and occurrences in a dream are accompanied by emotions, sometimes stronger than other times, but there is an interaction between the dreamer and the "show" he sees. Often people can be heard talking in their sleep, sometimes even shouting.

7. **Narrative to a plot.** Like a literary play, dreams always revolve around the narrative, even if it is unclear. Sometimes there is a combination of several dreams whose connection to each other is unclear, but to the dreamer they appear to be intertwined.

8. **Concentration and awareness.** While during the day – certainly in the digital age – a person is constantly distracted, when dreaming he is focused solely on his dream. The dreamer is immersed in the dream with no distraction by other issues.

TYPES OF DREAMS

Harry Hunt is someone who went to battle against the attempt to characterize dreams in a general way. In his book *The Multiplicity of Dreams: Memory, Imagination, and Consciousness*, Hunt divides dreams into various categories. Due to the variety of dreams, Hunt argues, any theory that tries to find common ground among all of them must be based only on certain types of dreams, choosing to ignore others. Thus, his approach is to look at dreams from a multi-dimensional perspective and select the means of treatment based on the type and category to which the dream belongs.

1. **Telepathic dreams.** Dreams in which information is transmitted between two people who are dreaming. Later we will discuss studies conducted over the years by Stanley Krippner and Montague Ullman regarding telepathy in dreams, including what exactly is possible to dream and transmit from the sender to the receiver of the dream.

2. **Archetypal dreams.** We discussed these dreams in the context of Jung's approach, which presents that there are archetypes in all people's psyches – universal patterns at the basis of all human behavior.

3. **Dreams that are works of art.** Mostly stemming from the dreamer's psyche. In these dreams, like in a work of art, figures and colors blend together and create visions and a script, as in a film with a director and producer.

4. **Dreams that reveal medical problems or physiological states.**

5. **Dreams that are characteristic of dreamers in dream laboratories.**

6. **Other types of dreams**. Dreams that cannot be rigidly categorized, and do not belong to any defined type. The need to create a general category of "other types" means that a patient cannot always be treated by a fixed pattern that must be applied according to type of dream, and indicates the realization that sometimes dreams cannot be categorized effectively.

OTHER TYPES OF DREAMS THAT DO NOT APPEAR ON HUNT'S LIST

7. **Lucid dreams.** A dream in which the person is aware, while dreaming, of the fact that it is a dream. Stephen LaBerge pioneered this field, and in the past two decades, many have chosen to continue on his path. In Israel, the leader in this area is the psychologist Udi Bonstein, who treats people via dreams and also wrote the book *Dreaming Full* on this subject. It is interesting to note that in the book, he points out that people in Israel remember more dreams than people in China, irrespective of the contents of the dream.

8. **Epileptic dreams.** Epilepsy is a neurological disorder that includes a tendency toward repeated seizures without any external cause. This disorder stems from abnormal and excessive activity of nerve cells in the cerebral cortex. There is a certain type of epilepsy in which the disorder and the attacks only occur in the limbic area of the forebrain, which creates some kind of emotional experience. When an epileptic attack takes place during sleep, dreams still occur, despite the fact that part of the brain is occupied with a different type of activity at the same time.

9. **Dreams and prophecy.** We will expand on this in the chapter on the philosophy of dreams. These dreams allow the dreamer an interface with a spiritual world; they include revelations and heavenly signs regarding phenomena or people as revealed during sleep.

MODERN THEORIES REGARDING THE PSYCHE AND OUR DREAMS

The Neurochemical Mechanism of Hobson and McCarley

Everything we have said up until now – even if it sounds familiar to you – is not necessarily universally accepted. In 1977, John Allen Hobson of Harvard University published an article in which he sought to challenge Freud's narrative regarding dreams. Yes, as you have already figured out, challenging and breaking conventions are part of scientific research in the psychological context as well. In his article, Hobson stated that there is a neurological basis to dreams, which take place via biochemical changes that the brain undergoes in order to enter REM, one of the stages of sleep. The biochemical flooding of the brain creates an encounter of neurons, which leads to the creation of images and feelings that appear in dreams. Hobson wrote the article after conducting a study on cats by implanting electrodes in their brain stems. In the study, Hobson and his colleague, Robert McCarley, a psychiatrist who collaborated with him, found that during alertness, serotonin (or HT-5), and noradrenaline (NA) were secreted in the cats; both are neurotransmitters that are produced in the brain stem. During REM, however, the cats secreted a different neurotransmitter: acetylcholine.

Accordingly, Hobson explains that the narrative we dream about is unconnected to the unique expression of the uncensored psyche. A dream is a biochemical process without any intrinsic meaning. Hobson negated the theories of both Jung and Freud and, in fact, all the psychologists who saw a dream as a window through which one could take a glimpse at the subconscious. Hobson bequeathed to us his innovative theory over the course of years through sleep labs, various writings such as his book *13 Dreams Freud Never Had*, and scientific journal articles that showed how subjects generated specific brain waves unrelated to the contents of the dream they were dreaming. Hobson's approach of course engendered many opponents, and even Hobson himself downplayed the implications of his own writings by revealing that he, too, kept a dream diary and that he saw significance in the things that appear in dreams, just not in their narrative sequence.

Ernest Hartmann and Dreaming as Psychotherapy

Ernest Hartmann was a researcher who investigated the biological aspects of REM sleep in an attempt to lay out what we know about dreaming. In his later research, Hartmann sought to prove that the dream process unfolds biologically via a model of a neural network involving connections that are created specifically during sleep and cannot be created in the waking state. In fact, functioning like an electrical circuit, these are neural connections that link various modules saturated with information while creating "connection" and "reconnection," which we experience as the sights and sensations of a dream.

In the waking state, use of that neural network is determined by the strength of the connections between the various units, while memory ties together all the connections on that network. During sleep, a phenomenon called "hyper-connectivity" occurs. That is, during dreaming we activate a broader range of possibilities via neural connections than we do while awake, and the lack of fixedness enables the wide variation in the dreams we experience.

Lavie and Israeli Research on the Holocaust, Dreams, and PTSD

Yes, Israel also has something to say about dreams. We have always been educated to dream, but it turns out that some Israelis have a unique addition to their dreams. The investigation of the existing relationship and dialogue with their dreams for those dealing with emotional distress and post-traumatic stress disorder (PTSD) has been led by Professor Peretz Lavie of the Technion. He focused his dream research on Holocaust survivors, discovering how traumatic events affect sleep and dreams via repression. In his studies, he compared Holocaust survivors to their peers who did not experience the war. In addition, he compared two groups of Holocaust survivors: those who remembered their war-related dreams, and those who did not. He found that those who did *not* remember actually reported a better quality of life than those who did remember them. This is the place for therapists and psychologists, whose job it is to provide an alternative to the repression mechanism in restraining the distress that the dreams and memories create during sleep.

It is interesting to note that a journalist named Charlotte Beradt investigated the subject of dreams between 1933 and 1939, until she was forced to flee from Europe to the United States. Twenty years later she published a book called *The Third Reich of Dreams*, in which she observed that there were dreamers who foresaw what Hitler was going to do, even though Hitler was just coming into power at the time. Are dreams prophesies of the future? Beradt didn't reach this unequivocal conclusion, but the dream descriptions in her book show a similarity between the Nazis' actions and Jews' dreams during that period.

Similarly, many survivors describe how dreams offered a sort of therapy in the difficult reality they were experiencing. Many survivors' dreams, some reported by the survivors themselves and others documented by psychologists in the Auschwitz-Birkenau Memorial and State Museum archives, show how prisoners in the concentration camps dreamed specifically about food and drink, dreams that helped them survive by providing them with hope and bodily pleasure. External stimulus? Hope? The researchers should hurry up because as the years pass, those survivors' time is waning.

Krippner and Ullman: Telepathy and Dreams

One claim that has been hovering around academia and various psychology and philosophy departments regards communication in dreams. This theory holds that two sleeping people can transfer information between them via telepathy. In the early 1970s, Professor Stanley Krippner of Saybrook University, in the U.S., investigated the feasibility of telepathy during dreams.

Krippner, realizing that he would not be able to prove this theory alone, collaborated with the psychiatrist Montague Ullman for 10 years. Together they initiated a series of experimental studies at the Maimonides Medical Center in New York to investigate the hypothesis that two people could communicate via a dream. Ullman and Krippner would divide the subjects into those whose job was to transmit the dream, and those whose job was to receive it. Transmission of the dream was done using an image that the sending dreamer was asked to study before sleeping. The researchers hoped that the image would stimulate an emotional and esthetic response in the dreamer, which could be transmitted telepathically. The sender and the receiver would meet before sleeping to become acquainted and interact briefly, and then they would be sent to separate rooms. While sleeping, both the sender and the receiver would be hooked up to electrodes; towards the end of the REM sleep, the researchers would actively awaken both sides and ask them to record a detailed report of what they saw in their dreams.

Krippner and Ullman succeeded in proving the existence of telepathy but were less successful in confirming it scientifically, i.e., to the extent that conclusions could be drawn about it. The existence of information transmission that may occur between two people during dreaming has been proven, but the nature of the process and how it occurs, along with the conditions required to cause it, remain scientifically hazy.

THE JAPANESE DREAM DICTIONARY AND HORIKAWA'S RESEARCH

It's true that we're still in the chapter on psychology, but as long as we're already discussing modern research, you must hear about the following study.

In 2013, a Japanese research team published the results of a dream study, during which the participants' dream fragments were recorded via an FMRI scanner and EEG instrument. The subjects recounted their dreams while the instruments showed all sorts of different electrical connections. Horikawa and his colleagues assembled a kind of dictionary in which each electrical connection was attached to a symbol or object appearing in a dream, and sent the participants to another test in which again they fell asleep and dreamed while the electrical activity in their brain was being monitored.

Next, after the subjects had dreamed, but before they were asked about their dreams, Horikawa and his colleagues tried to decode the dreams on the basis of decoding the test alone. They succeeded in revealing the contents of the dreams to varying extents, but not the identity of the dreamer or the emotion that the dream aroused in him.

They thus created an opening to future dream research, enabling researchers to get clear pictures of the signals that may create specific images appearing in dreams. In addition, after the decoding stage, it may be possible to implant dreams via electrical stimulation of certain areas of the brain that create good dreams or, alternatively, use drugs to quiet the parts that create nightmares during the night.

As in any good psychological treatment, the encounter never really ends; each meeting is an opportunity and a call for another meeting that is deeper and more aware. Psychology's focus in dream research is the understanding that it is primarily the dreamer – and not the dream – that should be analyzed. Breaking the dream down into components and identifying its characteristics can help categorize the dream and adapt the treatment to the dreamer and his dream.

Psychology and science go hand in hand, as we have seen in this chapter and will see in more depth in the next chapter. The former analyzes and breaks the problem down into components, while the latter creates better treatment tools. What they have in common is the understanding that we cannot ignore the dreams that visit us every night. To understand the innovations of science, we must enter the lab (after donning the required lab coat and gloves) and scientific academia in order to see how dreams are defined.

3

THE SCIENCE OF DREAMS

RAPID EYE MOVEMENT AND THE CHANCE DISCOVERY OF DREAMS

Dreams' entry into science could only have been as it happened – by chance. Yes, like many scientific discoveries, dreams were not the researchers' main interest when they were "discovered." Our story begins with a not-so-successful student by the name of Eugene Aserinsky who was failing his various subjects. After he had dropped out of four different degree programs, he enrolled at the University of Chicago to study physiology, and Nathaniel Kleitman was appointed to be his supervisor. Kleitman wanted to refute an article published in the journal *Nature* dealing with the rate of blinking during the stage of falling asleep, and his student Aserinsky was assigned to a tracking task, observing infants blinking. After a few weeks, Aserinsky's attempt to refute the study failed.

However, the student, who had always dreamed of breaking into the scientific world, suggested that the professor investigate not only the blinking but also the fluttering of the eyelids. Although not enthusiastic, Kleitman didn't stand in Aserinsky's way, permitting the student to conduct the research on his own son, Armand. By chance, Aserinsky began to discover that, despite the fact that his son fell asleep and gradually stopped blinking, there were still movements transmitted via electrodes attached to his head, making it appear as though he were still awake. Aserinsky decided to add a few more subjects – his wife and his daughters – to examine the phenomenon, and he discovered that indeed, for each one of the subjects, there was cognitive activity in the brain during the night, as though the sleeping subjects were behaving like they did during their waking hours.

In 1953 Kleitman and Aserinsky wrote an article on the phenomenon of dream sleep, which takes place in sleep cycles of between 90 and 110 minutes for adults, and between 30 and 45 minutes for infants. There are between four and five sleep stages, which can be divided into two main categories. The stages are integrated into cycles, joining various states that will be described below. The two broad categories of sleep stages are:

1. **Rapid Eye Movement (REM).** This stage appears only *once* in each sleep cycle. At this stage, one can observe noticeable eye movements and accelerated brain waves that transmit as they do during waking hours, and are sometimes even more active than in a person who is awake. The skeletal muscles are in a state of paralysis, blood pressure and blood supply to the brain increase, and the sleeping person reacts to changes in the surrounding environment. When the person is awakened while in the REM stage of sleep, he will remember his dream.

2. **Non-Rapid Eye Movement (NREM).** This stage appears in various sleep configurations in each cycle, when one can observe reduced brain activity, very slow brain waves, and a re- duction in respiration rate, blood pressure, pulse rate, and body temperature.

It should be noted that although the connection between REM and dreams is familiar to everyone, there are scientists who hold differing opinions. Mark Solms is a South African psychoanalyst and neuropsychologist known for discovering the brain mechanisms of dreaming and his use of psychoanalytic methods in contemporary brain science. He holds the chair of neuropsychology at the University of Cape Town and Groote Schuur Hospital (departments of psychology and neurology) and is president of the South African Psychoanalytical Association. Solms claims that he has managed to prove that there is no connection between dreaming and REM sleep. His proof of this lack of connection hangs on the fact that when sleepers are awakened during various stages of sleep, there is no significant difference between the types of dreams they report. James Pagel, a sleep researcher at the University of Colorado, has voiced a similar position, claiming no connection between dreams and REM, and that there are both dreams dreamt without REM and REM sleep during which the sleeper does not have any dreams.

THE SLEEP CYCLE AND THE GENERALLY ACCEPTED SCIENTIFIC THEORY TODAY

It is impossible to understand the science of dreams without explaining the sleep cycle. Here is a description of the sleep cycles and the appearance of dreams in non-technical language:

Throughout the 24-hour day, the body cyclically secretes the hormone cortisol, with cortisol levels in the blood rising in the morning, when a person is waking up, and diminishing in the evening, before sleep and as sleep begins. In addition, another hormone, melatonin, secreted by the pineal gland in the center of the brain, is activated at about nine in the evening. The levels of melatonin in the blood rise then, causing a lack of alertness and tiredness. In the morning, melatonin levels go down, causing a feeling of increasing alertness.

The sleep researcher William Dement made other significant discoveries about body and brain activity during sleep, through his study of subjects' eye movements using the electrooculogram (EOG). Here is a description of the sleep cycles as observed in Dement's and other studies

1. **Stage N1.** In this stage, characterizing the onset of sleep, eye movements slow down. The person is not yet entirely asleep and is still aware of what is happening around him, so it is easier to wake people up at this stage. This stage lasts an average of 10 minutes. The alpha waves emitted from the brain appear at a frequency between 8 and 12 Hz and begin to disappear.

2. **Stage N2.** This is the second stage of sleep, in which the subject's awareness of his environment disappears and he falls asleep. Theta waves are between 4 and 7 Hz and this stage of entering sleep is a stage in its own right, before the person becomes fully asleep. Stage 2 is responsible for half of the total night's sleep and therefore how one enters

this stage is important, both for NREM sleep and for dreaming. This stage lasts an average of 10 to 25 minutes.

3. **NREM** (also called N3 in the scientific literature). This is known as the stage of deep sleep. We spend about a quarter of our night's sleep in this stage, while it becomes shorter as we approach awakening (from 40 minutes per cycle at the beginning of the night to a few minutes as we approach awakening). The muscles are totally relaxed, body temperature is at a minimum, brain activity is controlled by an extremely slow wave (the delta wave – 1-4 Hz,) and there is almost no awareness of the surrounding environment.

4. **REM** (the dream stage). In this stage, brain activity sort of "wakes up" and there is evidence of increased alpha and the-ta waves. Despite the paralyzed muscles, the eye muscles and breathing act as they do in the waking state, alongside body temperature and heart rate, and eye movements occur rapidly. This is, as we noted, the stage in which dreaming occurs. This stage is responsible for a quarter of our total sleep, and it increases in length as we approach awakening (thus the longer dreams occur towards morning).

N1 → N2 → SLOW-WAVE SEEP NREM → N2 → REM (DREAM STAGE)

Aserinsky and Kleitman proved that dreams also appear in developed animals. Aserinsky was the first to actually discover the eye movements during dreaming and to apply modern tools to investigate the phenomenon of dreaming, but Kleitman was the one who headed the study and, together with his students, investigated other characteristics of sleep and dreams. His research led to the first sleep disorders clinic in 1970, at Stanford University, established by William Dement. Later, Kleitman was named the "father of scientific sleep research and of the physiology of dreams." Aserinsky, on the other hand, did not earn fame for himself, and continued his academic career in lesser-known universities. Apparently in science, as in other endeavors, it's not enough to be brilliant – you need a little luck as well.

LIGHT AND DARK: POLYPHASE SLEEP

If we are discussing cycles, we must also address day and night. Like everything else in our lives, sleep and dreams have been affected by the industrial and technological revolution. Human nature used to be in tune with the regular shifts between day and night, but with the onset of electric lighting, that is no longer the case. This change is reflected in currently accepted sleep patterns. There is evidence to show that before electric lighting became a permanent fixture in people's homes, the night's sleep was divided differently than it is now. The first part, which began shortly after sunset and was defined as the "first sleep," was followed by a waking period of an hour or two before the second part, which lasted until sunrise.

Historian Roger Ikritz notes many sources proving these sleep patterns, including Christian prayers that would be said during the waking period between the two sleep periods. Judaism has *tikkun hatzot* (midnight prayers) which took place between the two sleep periods. Other evidence can be found in personal diaries and physicians' books from the Middle Ages, recommending which foods can be eaten during the waking stage and how one should behave between the two sleep periods.

SLEEP DISORDERS

Sleep, which many of us take for granted, occupies a significant portion of our lives. There are those whose sleep is faulty or interrupted in undesirable ways. A lack of normal sleep cannot but harm dreams' integration into the sleep cycle. Sleep disorders are divided into three main categories, based on the stage in which they appear: "before sleep," "during sleep," and "when awakening from sleep."

1. **Insomnia disorders** (before sleep). These disorders are connected to the process of falling asleep or problems in the transition between sleep modes. This category includes difficulty falling asleep, waking up during the night between sleep cycles, and waking up early in the morning. This category also includes cyclical motor disorders, jerking of the muscles while falling asleep, talking in one's sleep, and leg cramps during sleep.

2. **Parasomnia sleep disorders** (during sleep). These disorders occur while a person is asleep. They include behavioral disorders connected to REM (sleep behavior disorders) such as walking or talking during sleep. Nightmares – dreams containing events that leave a difficult impression on the dreamer – also fall into this category. Other examples are sleep paralysis, painful erections during sleep, and heart rate disruptions (sinus arrest).

3. **Hypersomnia disorder** (when awakening from sleep). These disorders are connected to daytime sleepiness, in which the person does not manage to disconnect completely between sleep and wakefulness. In addition, some suffer from a breathing imbalance during sleep, and cannot regulate their breathing naturally in the various stages described above.

There are also sleep disorders that are not directly connected to sleep, but rather are symptoms of another physical or psychological problem in the person trying to sleep (such as disorders of the nervous system). Sleep disorders connected to psychological disorders can be found among those suffering from psychosis, depression, anxiety, panic attacks, and alcoholism. Sleep disorders connected to neurological disorders can be found among those suffering from degenerative brain disorders, dementia, Parkinson's, fatal familial insomnia, epilepsy during sleep, headaches during sleep, etc.

Some sleep disorders can be clearly identified because they result from use of some chemical compounds (including drugs), the simultaneous use of several types of compounds, or the sudden cessation of their use. These may be all sorts of illegal narcotics, permitted chemical compounds (such as caffeine, which is a stimulant, or alcohol), or physician-prescribed drugs that cause side effects.

Sleep problems can also be categorized by the character of the disorder, rather than according to sleep stages as shown above. Here are some such categories:

1. **Sleep disorders stemming from an internal source.** These disorders include those that can be shown to be caused by something within the person, such as insomnia, cyclical

hypersomnia, and sleep apnea, as well as leg syndromes affected by a dream.

2. **Sleep disorders stemming from an external source.**
   These relate to a sleeper's external environment and factors that disrupt his sleep. These disruptions can stem from his geographical location, lifestyle (such as alcohol consumption), taking stimulants, etc., as well as poor sleep hygiene.

3. **Sleep disorders connected to the biological clock.**
   A person's biological clock is programmed such that hormones are secreted or suppressed during sleep. Drastically changing one's normal pattern of alertness during the day and sleep at night can lead to sleep disorders. Thus, for example, shift work may confuse the biological clock and cause it to change. In addition, a familiar sleep disorder is caused by the transition between time zones, known as jet lag. This disorder does not merely disrupt one's regular sleep; it can also lead to depression and fatigue, or to an opposite reaction of excess adrenaline and a burst of gaiety. So the next time you're planning a meeting that involves flying, remember this research as well.

That's not all. It seems that the sleep disorder known as jet lag can have a far wider significance. In 1995, researchers Lawrence Recht, Robert Lew, and William Schwarz published a study on U.S. Major League baseball teams, in which they showed that teams that travelled eastward to away games won less frequently (37%) than those who travelled westward (44%). It was shown that the distance causes deterioration in personal skills and alertness. In light of this study, both business people and sports teams with meetings in distant countries began preparing several days before the meeting in order to prevent this state of temporary inferiority.

DON QUIXOTE SYNDROME

The Don Quixote syndrome, or in scientific language "REM Sleep Behavior Disorder," describes a person who is disconnected from reality and insists on fighting for his ideas, or alternatively is naïve about achieving a hopeless goal. Besides the philosophical meaning, the expression has gained a meaning relating to a wide range of medical symptoms that have even been translated to the world of sleep. Some claim that Don Quixote, Man of La Mancha, suffered from the sleep disorder that bears his name. The Don Quixote syndrome was discovered by the sleep researcher Michel Jouvet who, as early as 1979, by conducting surgery on cats, identified the location in the brain stem responsible for paralysis during sleep. It turns out that in the dreaming stage of sleep, despite the range of emotions and experiences, a person is prevented from moving; except for brain activity, the body is in a state of paralysis. However, sometimes the overlap between the sleeping state and the waking state is not the same for the brain and the body. Thus a situation is created in which the brain is awake but the body is sleeping.

Sometimes the opposite phenomenon appears. A weakening of the paralysis mechanism, which may appear among older people who respond to their dreams with bodily actions, may predict Parkinson's disease. Parkinson's, as noted, is typically diagnosed in the elderly, but can also appear in younger people, as a side effect of taking antidepressant drugs or for other reasons, and also appears frequently in narcolepsy sufferers.

SLEEP LABS

Sleep labs, also called "institutes of sleep medicine" have become more widespread in recent decades. Israel's pioneer of sleep research was Professor Peretz Lavie, who established a sleep lab in 1976. In 1980 this lab, in addition to conducting research, began diagnosing sleep problems and offering treatment for sleep disorders. Over the years, the State of Israel began recognizing sleep medicine institutes in accordance with the Ministry of Health brochure "Recognition of Institutes of Sleep Medicine" (brochure 7/2001). This brochure was issued after an investigation by a professional committee formed to evaluate institutes of sleep medicine.

In the U.S. there are currently more than 2,500 sleep labs. In addition, the American Academy of Sleep Medicine (AASM)[6] provides several information resources regarding sleep disorders, including dreamless sleep. Another prominent entity in the sleep field in the U.S. is the National Sleep Fund, a non-profit organization that promotes public understanding of sleep disorders. The National Sleep Fund website also includes a variety of resources on sleep and sleep disorders, including dreamless sleep.

STEPHEN LABERGE, LUCID DREAMING, AND THE MILD TECHNIQUE

Stephen LaBerge began his research on lucid dreams after the appearance of Celia Green's book, *Lucid Dreams*. While a PhD student at Stanford, LaBerge decided to write his thesis on the subject of lucid dreams. He joined William Dement, who had assisted in Aserinsky's research and was a sleep researcher with his own successes. LaBerge continued to study this field until he succeeded to not only demonstrate lucid dreaming on himself, but also to develop

---

6   https://aasm.com

a unique technique called MILD (Mnemonic Induction of Lucid Dreaming), which he presented in his book *Exploring the World of Lucid Dreaming*.

According to LaBerge's method, it is possible to achieve lucid dreaming via a technique that increases one's self-awareness during dreaming. In this technique, one must relate to the dream during the day as well, beginning with the stage of awakening, and deal with it intensively while awake. For example, the memory of the dream should be enhanced by recording it after getting up in the morning; during the day, while engaged in various activities, the person should periodically ask himself whether he is currently awake or dreaming. One must "get used to" searching for and evaluating those details in the dream that differ from reality, such as the appearance of the palms of the hands, reading of words (whether the reading is coherent or changes as it goes along), or the clock (whether time progresses consistently). This examination helps at a later stage, during the dream, to notice that one is in fact dreaming, while at the same time improving the clarity and lucidity of the dream.

Other stages take place during preparation for sleep, when the dreamer consciously prepares himself to dream and wants to remember the topic he would like to dream about. The last stage is for the person to imagine the dream or the scene that he wants to see in the dream and, using his imagination, to insert the items or people into the dream. The imagination stage is when the person falls asleep and begins to dream, until he reaches aware, lucid dreaming. LaBerge established the Lucidity Institute and began to publicize his method through various guide books. The researchers note that failing to use the dreaming and maintenance technique regularly will cause the frequency of lucid dreams to fall, eventually returning to the general norm.

DREAMLESS SLEEP SYNDROME

Most people do not remember their dreams. However, there are some people who do not dream at all. This is called the "dreamless sleep syndrome," and there are several diagnoses connected to the lack of dreaming. Dreamless sleep can be caused by disorders in brain activity during sleep, or internal bodily mechanisms that regulate dreams. Several studies have shown that dreamless sleep may be common among people suffering from PTSD. As with any other mystery, Israel has a unique contribution to make; this one arrived by chance, and it confused sleep researchers the world over.

In 1970, during Israel's War of Attrition, while doing his regular army service in Egypt's Great Bitter Lake region, Yuval Hamtzani suffered a near-fatal shrapnel injury to the brain. The motor injury from the wound left Hamtzani severely disabled but did not prevent him from becoming a lawyer, a gifted crossword puzzle maker, and an artist. Hamtzani claimed that from the time of his injury, his sleep was not accompanied by dreams. This contradicted the accepted scientific theory up until 1982, which held that there was no such thing as sleep without dreams.

Hamtzani was referred to the sleep lab of Professor Peretz Lavie, who found that during all sleep stages studied, virtually no dream sleep appeared, and even when it did appear, it was only a very small percent. Hamtzani's unique situation was even recorded in the *Guinness Book of World Records*, and mainly led to the exposure of a syndrome that science had yet to quantify: the phenomenon of people who do not dream. Despite his lack of dreams, Hamtzani continued to live without differing noticeably from people who do dream (Hamtzani died in March 2021 at age 71).

DREAM ENGINEERING

If we already understand dreams, why don't we engineer them? Like in ancient Greece, where people went to the temple in order to incubate dreams, dream engineering is coming back with a slightly different twist. While the worlds of therapy are trying to process dreams and decode them, the worlds of engineering and technology are trying to design our dreams and make them more effective. The desire to engineer dreams comes out of a sense that science has reached a dead end; up until now, it has only hypothesized the cause of dreams and the connection between health problems and lack of sleep, but has not provided a clear answer as to why dreams are so important for human beings.

The research team in the Media Lab of the prestigious Massachusetts Institute of Technology has developed a device called "Dormio." The process of "dream seeding" is conducted using a recording in which the dreamer states what he wants to dream about. The apparatus then identifies the awakening and dreaming stages and instructs the dreamer, via a sort of guided meditation, at just the moment before he enters the dream.

The engineering of dreams has drawn many opponents for a long time, based on the claim that a dream is a product of the subjective subconscious, and therefore any outside intervention is undesirable. However, the process of engineering dreams can help those who encounter nightmares and dreams that give them no rest. Likewise, we should remember that trauma victims often dream about the trauma over and over, and the process of dream engineering could help in their healing.

As of today, there is no effective treatment for nightmares except a drug called Prazosin, which is also used to treat high blood pressure, symptoms of enlarged prostate, and PTSD. The drug creates an artificial barrier to the adrenalin that the nightmares can stimulate, and also neutralizes norepinephrine (NE), which is rather hard to describe, so we will use the dictionary definition: "an excitatory neurotransmitter from the monoamine class, belonging to the catecholamine family." However, Prazosin can cause dizziness and fainting when getting up from lying down or sitting, as well as headaches and nausea.

In 2015, the well-known journal *Scientist* published a study in which a French research team tried to implant artificial memory in lab mice. They did so by focusing a beam of light on parts of the forebrain that are connected to the brain's pleasure reward centers and also affect the body. The study showed how after stimulation of the pleasure centers, when the mice entered a dream, their brains tried to stimulate those pleasure points again during sleep.

ANOTHER KIND OF DREAM – HYPNOPOMPOUS HALLUCINATION

There are those who think they are dreaming, but do not realize that they are actually in a psychotic state. This phenomenon was discovered by Frederic Myers, a British psychical researcher and poet (a winning combination for understanding the human soul) and one of the founders of the Society for Psychical Research. Even though his experiments and studies were not accepted by the scientific community of his time, Myers' work was revitalized in 2007 when a research team from the University of Virginia Medical School published empirical evidence proving his ideas about the subconscious and its influence. One of his definitions was that of a "hypnopompous hallucination," a hallucination that is felt by a person's senses without any external trigger. Thus Myers' dream about receiving recognition for hallucinations was fulfilled.

So how does this happen? Sometimes, as a result of increased activity of the central nervous system, a person experiences hallucinations that can stem from a psychotic state, psychological distress, illness, head injury, dehydration, use of stimulants, or more than three days without sleep. Some of the hallucinations appear with various colors and shapes as well as figures that generate a dialogue with the person hallucinating... Yes, just like in a dream.

In addition, there are hallucinations that have already earned official recognition, such as schizophrenia, in which the suffer- er experiences visual or auditory hallucinations. Another such disorder is bipolar disorder (manic depression), in which a disturbance of the emotional spectrum leads to disproportional responses. One criterion for diagnosing a hypomanic episode, according to the fifth edition of the *Diagnostic and Statistical Manual of Mental Disorders*, is a reduced need for sleep, which indicates a connection to sleep and its importance to the patient's response. Some of the hallucinations are experienced as a sort of waking dream in which the person is subject to a psychotic attack, in which he experiences difficulty distinguishing between reality and imagination.

However, there is a significant difference between a dream occurring during REM sleep and a hallucination that occurs while someone is awake. Hallucinations are usually treated with drugs whose function is to rebalance the person's nervous system and thus prevent the hallucinations. Dreams, in contrast, are unlikely to hurt the person or his environment.

FALSE AWAKENING

Have you ever had the experience of dreaming that you are awake, that you woke up from the dream? Confusing? It turns out this is a known phenomenon called "false awakening." The dreamer is convinced that he is awake, even though in reality he is continuing to sleep and dream. Celia Green, a British parapsychologist, has suggested that one should distinguish between two types of false awakening:

1. **False awakening in an imaginary environment.** In this type of awakening, the dreamer awakens in an imaginary environment, not in his bedroom. Dreamers who wake up in a false awakening will usually think that they are waking up and will fall back to sleep in the dream. Sometimes a false awakening is caused by panic or stress about fulfilling a task on the upcoming day. A notorious example of a characteristic false awakening of this type is bedwetting. The dreamer, believing that he is awake, relieves himself and awakens only after the bedwetting to discover that it was a false awakening in an imaginary environment.

2. **False awakening in a real environment.** In the second type, considered less common, the dreamer is characterized by a sense of tension or anxiety that makes this awakening feel like a hallucination. The person feels that there is something suspicious but cannot put his finger on the difference. Someone who has a false awakening in a real environment will perform the routine tasks that he does on awakening, but in the dream – such as brushing his teeth, relieving himself, showering, or cooking.

So what is a dream? An electrical system that screens shows in our heads? A natural phenomenon devoid of meaning? The influence of the nervous system and an attempt to discharge and clear the mind of the day's experiences? Science does not present a clear answer to this question. As usual, it deals with hypotheses and posits theories that can be contradicted as technology moves this research forward. But science mainly asks what the thing is and tries to understand how it is constructed. Humanity, however, is never satisfied with the "What" question, always immediately going on to ask, "Why?" These questions require us to enter the world of philosophy.

4

THE PHILOSOPHY
OF DREAMS

PHILOSOPHY AND DREAMS

Philosophy has wrought changes in almost everything that exists in the world. It has left its mark on all things, large and small, dissecting the human being and the world with a fine scalpel, so it is not surprising that dreams have also merited philosophical treatment. The fantastical, mystical interface that presents itself during dreams has tempted many philosophers to try to use their thinking patterns to crack the mystery of dreams. As in any philosophical discussion, we will begin at the beginning, in ancient Greece.

DREAMS IN ARISTOTLE'S TEACHINGS

As described in the introduction, the ancient Greeks ascribed both spiritual and medical significance to dreams. A work entitled *On Dreams*, ascribed to Hippocrates, who lived about 2,400 years ago, describes the dream as a powerful tool that could be used to diagnose various physiological diseases. Galen, a physician from the second century CE, also saw dreams as a healing tool, and wrote a work entitled *On Diagnosis from Dreams.*

Aristotle (384-322 BCE) was one of the most renowned philosophers of ancient Greece, and his ideas influenced and continue to influence Western philosophical thinking. He was a student of the famous philosopher Plato, and later even became the teacher of Alexander of Macedon. Aristotle dealt with a wide range of subjects that included metaphysics, ethics, philosophy, poetry, politics, playwriting, logic, physics, and others (and, in fact, he was responsible for delineating these fields of inquiry). It is not surprising that Aristotle also addressed the realm of sleep, waking, and dreams. He discussed these subjects in his *History of Animals*, in which he presents his theory that animals dream like humans.

According to Aristotle, one must distinguish between sleep and dreaming, even though they are in the same realm. Dreams activate the power of the imagination, but during sleep we lack our waking ability to judge fantasy, just as sick people lack this ability, and therefore in a dream we accept the imagined as real. For Aristotle, the power of imagination is a function of the soul, which is found between the purely bodily function and the purely intellectual function. On the one hand, during imagination it appears that we are looking at some physical object, but we are not experiencing the feeling of something real that we grasp with our senses, and so it is not an experience that we are physically aware of. On the other hand, the false impression of the imagination (and the dream) is also not true intellectually, since we cannot evaluate information and analyze its veracity during sleep.

Aristotle ranked dreams into levels. Among some animals one can notice that their eyelids move during sleep and therefore they are dreaming (regarding egg-laying animals, Aristotle claimed that he didn't know whether or not they dreamed). Among humans, there are different types of dreams. Aristotle explained that "The human is the most dreaming creature among all the animals" (*Aristotle's Anthropology*). In early childhood, humans sleep but do not dream. According to Aristotle, dreams begin at age four or five, and may begin to appear even later in some people.

One of Aristotle's most important claims about dreams was to refute the false opinion that it is the gods who send dreams. In his words, the very fact that dreams come to ordinary people and not only to the best and wisest, as well as the fact that animals dream, proves that this opinion is something that is "irrational and unthinkable." Aristotle goes on to state that dreams cannot prophesy future events, and even when they appear to, they are at most rare coincidences. However, Aristotle admits that such a coincidence is something supernatural, although not divine.

Aristotle related to dreams as a system of indications showing the specific bodily state of the dreamer. This description interfaces both with Freud's theories (as described above), and with theories in the Babylonian Talmud, as we will see later on. For Aristotle, dreams with many details, disturbances in a dream's continuity, or forgetting dreams, indicates that the dreamer is suffering from a functional disharmony. This, in a nutshell, is Aristotle's position on dreams, and he created an opening for later philosophers to deal with dreams.

DREAMS IN AVICENNA'S PHILOSOPHY

Philosophy is not only Greek. In fact, it is safe to say that much of philosophy's development can be credited to Islamic philosophers. One of these was Abū ʿAlī al-Ḥusayn bin ʿAbdullĀh ibn al-Ḥasan bin ʿAlī bin Sīnā, known as Avicenna, who was heavily influenced by the Greeks and by Aristotle in particular. Avicenna was born in 980 CE and died at the age of 57. Despite his relatively short life, he managed to earn a reputation as a famous scientist not only in Islam but in the history of all humanity. Avicenna was physician to the Sultan and even cured him of a dangerous illness in 997. As a reward for his abilities, he was granted access to the Samanid Royal Library, and thus he expanded his knowledge and had a significant advantage over others who were involved in science. The fact that this library later burned down caused speculation that perhaps he was involved in setting the fire in an attempt to gain an advantage over other people.

Besides writing some 450 books, mostly dealing with medicine and philosophy, Avicenna also found time to treat people with aromatherapy oils. His philosophic theory is still studied in philosophy departments throughout the world, and his image still lingers over sites, street names, and statues, mostly in Iran. One work attributed to him is the *Epistle on Dreams*, which reflects the medieval concept that a dream is derived from the structure of the dreamer's personality and his intellectual knowledge (it should be noted that many researchers question the attribution of this epistle to Avicenna).

In the epistle, Avicenna divides dreams into four types: The first three do not belong to divine power but rather are images found within the power of the imagination, and they are assembled and dismantled according to what the person desires during sleep. Avicenna observed that people often dream about imaginary, false images that belong to that fourth, divine category, but he called these baseless hallucinations such as those seen by mentally ill people or those suffering from a high fever:

1. **First type.** Stems from a change of spiritual temperament (influence on the soul as the result of a particular experience), and takes place in the forebrain.

2. **Second type.** Stems from the power of the imagination; exposure to this dream remains in the imagination and does not dissipate. That is, the person is exposed to an experience during the day and it becomes "stuck" in his brain, creating a sense of reality for the dreamer.

3. **Third type.** Also stems from the power of imagination: When the person purposefully reflects before sleep, he will dream about what he was reflecting on, since the reflection has not yet dissipated.

4. **Fourth type.** This is the "prophetic-divine" dream.

While Aristotle chose to disconnect the gods from dreams, creating a scale that moved from natural through supernatural to divine, Avicenna saw a connection between dreams and God. He saw dreams as a vehicle for an interface between two intelligences: According to the dreamer's intellectual capacity, he is exposed to God's goodness and to information regarding future events that appear in the dream. According to Avicenna, there is a difference between an evil dream, in which the dreamer's exposure to the evil thing is close to the occurrence of the calamity, and a dream about good tidings, in which the dream's fulfillment is at a far remove from the time of the dream, due to God's desire to increase the joy of anticipation.

Note that many thinkers confused Aristotle's teachings with those of Avicenna, and ascribed the concept of the prophetic-divine dream to Aristotle. Thus, for example, the philosopher Shem Tov Ibn Falaquera, a commentator on Maimonides, as well as the Spanish philosopher Zarchia ben Yitzhak ben Shaltiel, both quoted Aristotle, from his book *Sense and Sensibilia,* and related to dreams as prophetic-divine. This is despite Aristotle's words, as quoted above, stating explicitly that something possessed by animals as well as humans cannot be divine.

DREAMS IN IBN RUSHD'S PHILOSOPHY

Avicenna was definitely not the last to engage with dreams and their philosophical aspects. Ibn Rushd (1126-1198) was a twelfth-century Islamic philosopher from Spain, who was known primarily as a commentator on Aristotle's writings. The fact that Ibn Rushd was devoutly religious did not prevent him from interpreting Aristotle, even when Aristotle's philosophy diverted religion and its ideas from the intellectual path. When he categorized dreams according to Aristotle's theory, Ibn Rushd distinguished between a correct dream and a false dream but avoided mentioning the prophetic dream.

Ibn Rushd explained that sorcery, prophecy, and dreams all share something in common, in that they all deliver some kind of content. In contrast to the popular belief that the content of each one came from a different source – prophecy from God, dreams from angels, and sorcery from demons –– Ibn Rushd believed that the difference lay in the quality of the content. He held that prophecy provides intellectual-scientific content, connected to an educated person's attainment of philosophical happiness, which is wisdom. In contrast, sorcery and dreams are independent of a person's desires, but their purpose is to transmit content related to his future.

According to Ibn Rushd, the ability to receive or, most correctly, to "absorb" a prophetic dream is linked to a person's physical temperament and not his intellectual temperament. His theory of temperament was developed from the early theory of the physician Hippocrates, who believed that there were four basic humors or fluids in the body, and that an imbalance between them could lead to injury. The temperament theory of Galen and Aristotle categorized people by their individual temperaments, according to four colors: red, white, yellow, and black. The black temperament, according to Ibn Rushd, was what allowed a prophetic dream to become established in a person.

Like Aristotle, Ibn Rushd believed that the imagination was primarily responsible for the contents of dreams, unrelated to the question of whether it was a prophetic and correct dream or a false dream. Given that awareness in the dream is disconnected from the environment that the person is exposed to while awake, a false dream can come either from the power of imagination or from a desire or lust of the dreamer. Ibn Rushd managed to unite the dream under a single roof that sheltered both philosophy and religion, and give it his unique interpretation, interweaving Aristotle and Islam together.

DREAMS IN MAIMONIDES' PHILOSOPHY

Maimonides, Rabbi Moshe ben Maimon (1138-1204), is considered one of the greatest adjudicators of Jewish law and one of the most important philosophers of the Middle Ages. In his halachic, philosophical, and medical writings, he encompassed almost the entire scope of important spiritual, halachic (referring to Jewish law derived from the Torah and Talmud), and intellectual issues that might concern a person. Maimonides corresponded with philosophers of his generation and presented clear theses on all the important scientific and philosophical concepts of his era.

Maimonides' philosophy on dreams should be drawn entirely from three sources: various places in the *Guide for the Perplexed*, the *Book of the Commandments*, and Jewish laws summarized in his *Mishneh Torah*. In a number of places, Maimonides notes that the expression of dreams is metaphoric and is not intended to be a prophetic vision, that the "real prophets" are different than those who lack logic and wisdom, and have only imagination and conjectures.

> *...but the phrase, "And Elohim (an angel) came to a certain person in the dream of night," does not indicate a prophecy, and the person mentioned in that phrase is not a prophet; the phrase only informs us that the attention of the person was called by God to a certain thing, and at the same time that this happened at night. For just as God may cause a person to move in order to save or kill another person, so He may cause according to His will, certain things to rise in man's mind in a dream by night. We have no doubt that the Syrian Laban was a perfectly wicked man, and an idolater; likewise Abimelech, though a good man among his people, is told by Abraham concerning his land [Gerar] and his kingdom, "Surely there is no fear of God in this place" (Gen. 20:11). And yet concerning both of them, viz., Laban and Abimelech, it is said [that an angel appeared to them in a dream]. Comp. "And Elohim (an angel) came to Abimelech in a dream by night" (ibid. ver. 3); and also, "And Elohim came to the Syrian Laban in the dream of the night." (ibid. 31:24)*[7]

---

7   Maimonides, *Guide for the Perplexed*, Part 2:41, English translation Michael Friedlander, 1903 (London: Routledge and Sons).

Maimonides believed that a "real" dream was a rare event, asserting that the chances of someone who is not a prophet seeing the truth in his dream are almost nil. Maimonides explained that even when dreams came to biblical figures who were not prophets, those dreams were not the product of divine revelation, but rather the work of the power of imagination. This also influences Maimonides' attitude towards idol-worshippers, such as the "Sabians," who would eat blood in an attempt to connect to demons. Maimonides said that this was not a true dream, but just imagination and hallucinations. For this reason, he explained, it is forbidden to eat blood, due to the Sages' concern that people would fall into idolatry and demon worship.

Maimonides clung to his position that dreams are a product of the imagination and not truth when he related to the prohibition on "gaining knowledge from the dead," a practice that is forbidden to Jews. This is not only a religious prohibition, but also, according to Maimonides, the practice is a mistake that bring a spirit of impurity, causing people to imagine false things, and not, in fact, revelations of the dead.

Maimonides thus illustrates the familiar approach we see in biblical verses in relation to dreams. Dreams are viewed negatively except when they appear in connection with the prophets who communicate with God through dreams. In Ecclesiastes, only fools put their hope in dreams: "For a dream cometh through a multitude of business; and a fool's voice through a multitude of words" (5:2); "For through the multitude of dreams and vanities there are also many words." (5:6)[8] The prophet Zechariah also connects dreams to sorcerers and false prophets when he says, "For the *teraphim*[9]

---

8   Here and for the rest of the book, unless indicated otherwise, all quotes from the Bible are taken from the English translation of the Jewish Publication Society, 1917
9   A kind of sculpture

have spoken vanity, and the diviners have seen a lie, and the dreams speak falsely, they comfort in vain; therefore they go their way like sheep, they are afflicted, because there is no shepherd." (10:2)[10] Maimonides related to dreams differently than other philosophers in general, and religious Jewish thinkers in particular. As we will see in the next chapter, the Hebrew Bible hints at an attitude towards dreams that sees them as a unique mystical experience, but one that also poses some kind of danger, even though the dreams themselves are imaginary.

Philosophy throughout the world accompanies man in these mixed feelings about dreams. It does not ignore the fact that there are many limitations on our ability to understand dreams, and that there are many dreams that are meaningless and impossible to interpret. Some have sought to view dreams as a bridge to another world; others have tried to see them as a means of transmitting content, with receipt of the content dependent on the dreamer's spiritual level; still others have viewed dreams as merely false imagination. Whichever philosophical theory you choose, one thing is clear to philosophers themselves: One cannot ignore dreams and their influence.

From philosophy we now delve into Judaism, to a religion that combines history and culture, laws and mysticism, and has given the world the greatest bestseller of the last 2,000 years: the Bible.

---

10   English translation: Mechon Mamre https://mechon-mamre.org/p/pt/ pt2310.htm

5

THE TORAH OF DREAMS: ON DREAMS IN THE BIBLE

Dreams appear many times throughout the Bible. In the Book of Genesis alone, the first of the 24 books, the root "ḥ-l-m"(dream) appears 48 times. Dreams weave through the Bible stories, adorning them with flashes of color. These biblical dreams are rooted in reality, particularly in the way they interface with divine revelation. Yet the Sages note differences among the various dreamers, precisely specifying how each dreamer received the dream, including the process of entering the realm of sleep.

Dream and prophecy are intertwined in the Bible; Deuteronomy 13:2 likens them, "If there arise in the midst of thee a prophet, or a dreamer of dreams." In Numbers as well, we find that God says of Himself that "I do speak with him in a dream," and the Talmud notes that a dream is one-sixtieth of prophecy (Berachot 57). Yet among the later prophets, like Jeremiah, we find that a dream becomes synonymous with vanity and nonsense. The Sages sanction this view with a warning about dreams' unreliability, directing people to maintain significant skepticism about the contents of a dream, keeping in mind that a dream may likely be no more than a meaningless fancy (Berachot 55; Nedarim 8). Did the Sages take this stance due to the lack of prophecy in that period? Or perhaps because dreams were increasingly being used for the wrong motives? Even though we have no clear answer to these questions, one can sense the difference between dreams in the Bible and dreams as they appear in the Babylonian Talmud and the various Jewish halachic texts.

ADAM'S DREAM

"And the LORD God caused a deep sleep to fall upon the Man, and he slept; and He took one of his ribs, and closed up the place with flesh instead thereof." (Genesis 2:21)

The creation of Woman does not happen while primordial Man is awake. Rather, he falls into a deep sleep and while he is unconscious, his rib is removed and Woman is created. The commentators Abarbanel and the Malbim, two Jewish rabbis who interpreted the Bible, explain that this sleep was the "very deep sleep" that is parallel to the states of sleep we are familiar with from science, as described in preceding chapters. The Babylonian Talmud (Sanhedrin 39) includes a dialogue between Rabban Gamliel and a heretic who accuses God of being a thief, since He took the rib while Adam was asleep. The Talmud describes how Rabban Gamliel's daughter seeks to answer the heretic with the example of cooking a steak over embers. Someone who observes the preparation stage would experience revulsion and therefore not find the end result appetizing. She explains that this was the reason for creating Eve while Adam was asleep. As a side note, there is no mention of Adam's awakening from this deep sleep, although we have not exhaustively addressed this issue.

Adam's deep sleep also affords us a unique look at sleep itself. A *midrash*, a rabbinic interpretation of the Hebrew Bible, (Yalkut Shimoni) notes that there are three types of unconsciousness:

> *"Three types of unconsciousness are: unconsciousness of sleep, "And a deep sleep fell on him;" unconsciousness of prophecy, "And a deep sleep fell on Avram;" and unconsciousness of a marmot's sleep, "No man saw it, nor knew it, neither did any awake; for they were all asleep; because a deep sleep from the LORD was fallen upon them." And some say even an unconsciousness of stupidity, "For the LORD hath poured out upon you the spirit of deep sleep, and hath closed your eyes." Three types of surrogates are: the surrogate for death is sleeping, the surrogate for prophecy is a dream, and the surrogate for the World to Come is the Sabbath. And some say: the surrogate for the heavenly light is the disk of the sun, the surrogate for heavenly wisdom is the Torah. (Yalkut Shimoni, Bereishit)*

Although Yalkut Shimoni is not discussing a dream here, it is certainly possible to draw an analogy between the types of deep sleep described and types of dreams. As we will see further on, the Sages have a complex relationship with dreams. As noted above, the Babylonian Talmud, in Berachot 47, states that the dream is "one-sixtieth of prophecy." Elsewhere it is stated that all dreams follow the mouth (Berachot 55-56), and according to Ecclesiastes (5:6), "For through the multitude of dreams and vanities there are also many words." Yalkut Shimoni's division of types of unconsciousness can also shed light on types of dreams. That is, a dream stems from a type of unconsciousness that seizes a person. The degree of unconsciousness and its quality depend not only on the person's level, but also on a decision from above, from where the unconsciousness is cast upon the person.

There are books and writings from ancient times, known as "pseudepigrapha," that were not included in the Bible due to various considerations. One of these is The Book of Adam and Eve, which describes the history of Adam and Eve in 43 chapters, starting from their expulsion from the Garden of Eden and up until Eve's death and burial next to Adam and Abel. This book describes Eve's dreams, in which she sees Abel's blood "spilled by Cain his brother and he drank it without mercy" (1:2). Eve tells Adam the dream, and the dream causes her to search for her two sons and, as a result, to discover that Abel was murdered by his brother. Another related dream appears to Adam in this book, in which the angel Michael appears to him and tells him that another son will be born to them to replace Abel. Nevertheless, Eve mourns Abel for her entire life. Later they have another son, named Seth; in total, they give birth to 30 sons and 30 daughters.

ENOCH'S DREAMS

Another pseudepigraph is the Book of Enoch, describing the history of Enoch, son of Yered and father of Methuselah. In the Bible, Enoch is described as someone who "walked with God" and after 365 years he disappeared because "the Lord took him," without the phrase "he died" that usually appears in the Book of Genesis. His devotion to God, and the ambiguity surrounding his death, led to several pseudepigrapha that describe him as turning into an angel, holding a dialogue with God, and transmitting the knowledge thus gleaned to human beings over the course of 30 days. Christians saw the Book of Enoch as prophecy and canonized it. Islam also accords honor to Enoch, mentioning him in the Koran by the name "Idris" and describing him in Islamic tradition as someone who rose to "a great height."

At present there are three known Books of Enoch, which are in fact versions that were found in different places and at different times:

1. **Enoch 1.** The pseudepigraph to the Bible, which was written in Aramaic and served as the inspiration for other pseudepigrapha such as the *Book of Jubilees, the Book of Giants, Testaments of the Twelve Patriarchs*, and others. The unusual spiritual significance that was attributed to Enoch made the rabbis reluctant to include this book in the Bible, even making efforts to suppress those who tried to follow it. This book was discovered at a very late stage, only in the eighteenth century, when James Bruce, a Scottish explorer, returned from Ethiopia with three copies in the Ge'ez language. In the 1950s, when the Dead Sea Scrolls were discovered, extensive sections from the Aramaic original were found. The Book of Enoch describes Enoch's greatness and his prophetic abilities, at the same time portraying human history from its beginning to the final redemption – when light will conquer darkness. In that redemption, God will reveal to the righteous "the chosen one"/"the man" (the Messiah) along with bringing the evil spirits and the "Nephilim" to justice.

2. **Enoch 2.** Preserved only in ancient Church Slavonic. The book was found in 1886 by the biblical researcher Nahum Sokolov in the public library of Belgrade.

3. **Enoch 3.** Written in Hebrew, variously named *The Third Book of Enoch, The Book of the Palaces,* and *The Book of Rabbi Ishmael the High Priest.* The book is a sort of continuation of Enoch 1 and appears to have been inspired by that book. Enoch 3 emphasizes Enoch's rise to heaven and his transformation into the angel Metatron.

Enoch 1 features a description of visions revealed to Enoch while he was awake, and other visions revealed to him while he slept.

> *...reading the memorial of their prayer, until I fell asleep. And behold a dream came to me, and visions appeared above me. I fell down and saw a vision of punishment, that I might relate it to the sons of heaven, and reprove them. When I awoke I went to them.... I related in their presence all the visions which I had seen, and my dream;* (Enoch 1 13:8-10)[11]

ABIMELECH'S DREAM

> *But God came to Abimelech in a dream of the night, and said to him: "Behold, thou shalt die, because of the woman whom thou hast taken; for she is a man's wife."* (Genesis 20:3)

Abimelech was the Philistine King of Gerar, and according to the Bible, the first dream appeared to him of all people. When Abraham decided to live among the Philistines, they were interested in his wife Sarah. Abraham, who was aware of Sarah's beauty, asked her to say that she was his sister so that things would go better for them. Abimelech's servants took Sarah to the king's dwelling, and in Abimelech's dream, God revealed Himself and warned the

---

11   English translation:https://book-ofenoch.com/chapter-13/

king that if he did not set the married Sarah free to return to her husband, he would be punished. Although Abimelech was angry with Abraham for lying and telling Sarah to pass as his sister, the king granted him great wealth as compensation for taking her.

It should be noted that from the Biblical text we understand that Abimelech acted innocently, given Sarah's declaration. However, commentators saw Abimelech in a less favorable light than the first impression from reading the biblical story. They emphasize that Abimelech took Sarah by force, and although they find that his act was innocent, they indicate that he lacked integrity. Commentators add that God chose to appear to Abimelech in a dream not because of his greatness, but in fact because of the greatness of Abraham, just as Abraham appeared in Laban's dream also. The Ralbag (Levi ben Gershon, also known as Gersonides) explains that Abimelech's dream was not "a dream about prophecy," but a dream that was "of the rank of accurate dreams," when he was shown his future punishment if he did not return Sarah to her husband.

A similar event takes place with Abraham's son, Isaac. When famine strikes the Land of Canaan, Isaac avoids leaving the Land of Israel, choosing instead to live in Gerar. In this case, Isaac, too, tells the local people that his beautiful wife is his sister, out of fear that they will try to kill him and take Rebecca. This time Abimelech is cautious, in no hurry to take her, perhaps due to his previous experience; over time, he sees or figures out that Rebecca and Isaac are in fact married, due to the expression of affection between them – "Isaac was sporting with Rebecca his wife." (Genesis 26:8) He summons Isaac and rebukes him for saying that Rebecca was his sister, almost causing Abimelech to sin with Rebecca. Isaac justifies himself by saying that he lied out of fear that he would be killed, and Abimelech accepts his apology. After rebuking him once more,

"What is this thou hast done unto us? One of the people might easily have lain with thy wife, and thou wouldest have brought guiltiness upon us" (Genesis 26:10), the king publicly announces that Isaac has royal protection, and that anyone who harms him or his wife will be put to death.

Nachmanides (Genesis 26:1) wonders whether the Abimelech in the story about Avraham is the same Abimelech in the story about Isaac, or whether perhaps all Philistine kings were named Abimelech, since the Philistine king in David's time was also named Abimelech. Nachmanides shares Onkelos' opinion that the Abimelech of Isaac's time was the son of Abraham's Abimelech. The Radak (David Kimchi) also took the position that it was not the same Abimelech. In contrast, Rabbeinu Bachya is not bothered by the chronological gap and holds that the same Abimelech appeared in both stories.

ABRAHAM'S DREAMS

The dream of the Covenant Between the Pieces was the first dream bearing national significance to appear to the Patriarch Abraham, even before the letter "h" was added to his name:

> *And the birds of prey came down upon the carcasses, and Abram drove them away. And it came to pass, that, when the sun was going down, a deep sleep fell upon Abram; and, lo, a dread, even a great darkness, fell upon him. And He said unto Abram: 'Know of a surety that thy seed shall be a stranger in a land that is not theirs, and shall serve them; and they shall afflict them four hundred years; and also that nation, whom they shall serve, will I judge; and afterward shall they come out with great substance. But thou shalt go to thy fathers in peace; thou shalt be buried in*

> *a good old age. And in the fourth generation they shall come back*
> *hither; for the iniquity of the Amorite is not yet full.'...In that*
> *day the LORD made a covenant with Abram, saying: 'Unto thy*
> *seed have I given this land, from the river of Egypt unto the great*
> *river, the river Euphrates.* (Genesis 15:11-16,18)

Abraham's dream was no ordinary dream. In it, both personal and communal promises are expressed, as well as tidings of his continuity, and even the making of a covenant. Abraham's deep sleep recalls the deep sleep of primordial Man before his rib was removed to form Woman. In both cases, the sleeping human is passive, but reality afterwards is never the same.

During the prayers read on Mondays and Thursdays, in the section *"V'hu rahum"* (and He is merciful), Jews ask God to "remember and look on the Covenant between the Pieces." Since this covenant also promises Israel's exile to Egypt and their enslavement there, it is unclear why we ask God to remember it again. The Covenant Between the Pieces expresses not only historical facts, but also a covenant in which those who follow Abraham's path are promised the Land of Israel from the Nile to the Euphrates.

THE DISPUTE BETWEEN MAIMONIDES AND NACHMANIDES

One of the most prominent disputes among Biblical commentators and Jewish thinkers is the dispute over some of the events described in the Book of Genesis, such as the angels who announce to Abraham the birth of his son, as well as the overthrowing of Sodom and Gemorrah. These interweave several basic points in Jewish thought, including the relationship to angels and human beings' capacity to communicate with them, as well as the relationship to dreams and to prophecy. Maimonides notes these things in several places, addressing them directly in his *Guide for the Perplexed*:

> *We have explained that wherever it is mentioned that an angel was seen or had spoken, this has happened only in a vision of prophecy or in a dream whether this is explicitly stated or not... And there is no difference between a statement in which the prophet literally affirms from the first that he saw the angel and a statement according to whose external sense the prophet at first thought that a human individual had appeared to him, whereas at the end it became clear to him that it was an angel... when speaking of the text of the Torah: And the Lord appeared unto him by the Terebinths of Mamre, and so on... that it too is a description of what he said in a vision of prophecy... I say likewise also of the story about Jacob in regard to its saying, "And there wrestled a man with him"... All the wrestling... happened in a vision of prophecy. And likewise the whole story of Balaam on the way and of the she-ass speaking; all this happened in a vision of prophecy, as it is finally made clear that an angel of the Lord spoke to him.*
> (Guide for the Perplexed, Section 2, Chapter 42)[12]

That is, according to Maimonides, the angels' visit to the Patriarch Abraham, like the story of the Patriarch Jacob's wrestling with the angel, did not happen in the physical realm, as one might conclude from the text. According to him, these events did not actually occur, but were only seen in a prophetic vision.

In contrast to Maimonides, Nachmanides in his commentary on the Book of Genesis (Genesis 18:1), after raising several ques-

---

12 English translation by Shlomo Pines https://archive.org/details/ MaimonidesGuide/page/388/mode/2up

tions, states that Maimonides' commentary is unclear. Why does the Bible need to precisely describe the encounter with the angels if everything was in a prophecy? Jacob's limp is described as something real – could he be limping from an injury that occurred solely in a dream? Thus Nachmanides concludes that what Maimonides wrote is incorrect and even calls it "words that contradict the written text and are forbidden to listen to them even if one does not believe them." It should be noted that Rabbi David Cohen, the Nazir, explains that Nachmanides lived in a Christian environment and was particularly sensitive to the possibility of Christians exploiting Maimonides' commentary. They might hear that a typical Jewish commentator explains that God revealed himself in the image of three people, and use it to claim belief in the Trinity. Maimonides, in contrast, operated in a Muslim environment in which this fear did not exist, and instead he was called on to fight folk superstitions that tended to seek spirituality in the form of demons and spirits. His faith mission obligated him to publicize the abstract character of the encounter with the angels.

The end of the story of Sodom and Gemorrah seems to reinforce Maimonides' approach:

> *Then the LORD caused to rain upon Sodom and upon Gomorrah brimstone and fire from the LORD out of heaven; and He overthrew those cities, and all the Plain, and all the inhabitants of the cities, and that which grew upon the ground. But his wife looked back from behind him, and she became a pillar of salt. And Abraham got up early in the morning...*(Genesis 19:24-27)

Why does the story need to end with Abraham getting up early in the morning? How is this connected to the events of Sodom and Gemorrah? Although Maimonides did not address this ending, it does seem to add weight to his position.

The fourteenth-century Spanish commentator Rabbi Yom Tov ben Avraham Ishbili (known by his initials as the Ritva), in *The Book of Remembrance*, tries to resolve Nachmanides' challenge to Maimonides. He explains that Nachmanides had not read *The Guide for the Perplexed* in depth because of his great diligence in the Talmud and "true wisdom," and therefore he interpreted Maimonides differently. According to the Ritva, even if the angels' visits were prophecy, it is not strange that there is a detailed description of other items. He adds that the dream could have left such a significant impression on Jacob that it even caused a physical limp, somewhat like a person who awakens perspiring from a bad dream. That is, the Ritva explains that Jacob's limp was caused by his prophetic vision while sleeping.

Another interesting commentary connected to our topic is the position of the fourteenth-century French commentator Levi ben Gershon, also known as Gersonides or Ralbag, who chose to resolve Nachmanides' challenge to Maimonides regarding Jacob's limp in a different way:

> It is possible that from all Jacob's labor in carrying all his possessions through the river, that while he was asleep the pain in his thigh renewed itself. And it seemed to him in the prophetic dream that he was wrestling with that man and that his thigh was injured in the wrestling with him, according to his wrestling that appeared to him. (Gersonides on Genesis 32, 33)

Gersonides follows the approach of Alfred Maury, according to which the pain Jacob felt caused him to see a vision in the dream.

That is, what a person feels before entering a dream or prophecy has an external influence on the dream or prophecy. Gersonides explains that the three people who came to Abraham were in fact people – that is, prophets – who came to bring tidings of Sarah's remembrance and of the sentence against Sodom. "Angels," then, was read as a term of honor, fitting for God's prophets.

JACOB'S LADDERS AND DREAMS

And he dreamed, and behold a ladder set up on the earth, and the top of it reached to heaven; and behold the angels of God ascending and descending on it. (Genesis 28:12)

During Jacob's journey northward, from Beersheba to Haran, he lay down to sleep under some rocks in the area of the village of Luz, and in his dream a ladder was revealed to him with angels who were ascending and descending. There are a number of different interpretations for the figures of the angels and what they symbolize:

1. The history of the Jewish people. The angels symbolize the rising and falling of world powers (Midrash Tanhuma, Ba'al HaTurim).

2. The connection between God and the human being. The angels symbolize the prayers and the sacrifices (Da'at haMikra).

3. Man's life in the world. The connection between the spiritual and physical world (Ba'al Shem Tov).

During the dream, God also appears to Jacob and promises

him the land that he is lying on. After he awakens, described as awakening from sleep, Jacob is deeply moved by his dream and announces that the place where he slept is the House of God and the gateway to Heaven, naming the place *Beit El* (House of God) (some believe that this refers to the present-day settlement of Beit El). Despite his declaration, Jacob vows that if the dream indeed comes true, he will make the place a house of God and dedicate 10 percent of his possessions to charity. The Zohar (Genesis 150:2) wonders why Jacob needs to make a vow "if God will be with me;" was not everything that occurred in the dream enough? The Zohar answers in the name of Rabbi Yehuda that since the events occurred during a dream, there are some dreams that are true and others that are not. Therefore, when Jacob says, "if God will be with me," it does not indicate doubt, but rather a desire to instill meaning into the dream by virtue of God's name.

While all other dreams that appear in the Bible are accompanied by their interpretations, Jacob's dream about the ladder placed on the ground and reaching heavenward remains without interpretation in the biblical text.

The motif of the ladder in the semantic-kabbalistic context does not appear only in Jacob's dream. Ba'al Hasulam (whose name means "author of *The Ladder*"), or Rabbi Yehuda Leib Ha-Levi Ashlag (1884-1954), was a kabbalist and commentator on the Zohar. He was known as Ba'al Hasulam after the name of his commentary, *Hasulam* (The Ladder). Besides being a kabbalist, he was also a composer and was ordained as a rabbi and judge during his time in Warsaw before immigrating to Israel. Rabbi Ashlag was appointed by Rabbi Kook, then Chief Rabbi of British Mandatory Palestine, to be the rabbi of Givat Shaul. Rabbi Ashlag saw the ladder not only as a commentary but also as a way of life. In his approach, one could not advance spiritually without a kabbalistic rabbi who had achieved spiritual heights. One climbed higher spiritually only via those already located high up, as though on a ladder or a step.

Jacob continues to dream. In the Book of Genesis we find descriptions of the future-telling dream in which Jacob receives guidance from the angel on how to act when he leaves Laban:

> *And it came to pass at the time that the flock conceived, that I lifted up mine eyes, and saw in a dream, and, behold, the he-goats which leaped upon the flock were streaked, speckled, and grizzled. And the angel of God said unto me in the dream: Jacob; and I said: Here am I. And he said: Lift up now thine eyes, and see, all the he-goats which leap upon the flock are streaked, speckled, and grizzled; for I have seen all that Laban doeth unto thee. I am the God of Beth-el, where thou didst anoint a pillar, where thou didst vow a vow unto Me. Now arise, get thee out from this land, and return unto the land of thy nativity.* (Genesis 31:10-13)

Laban also has a dream as he is pursuing Jacob after his son-in-law fled from him. Midrash Tanhuma (Parshat Vayetze, Section 12) states that God chose to "make the pure impure" and reveal Himself to Laban for the sake of the righteous, as He did with Abimelech, when He warned the king not to have sexual relations with Sarah because she was married.

Another pseudepigraph is called the *Book of Testaments of the Twelve Patriarchs*, containing a book for each tribe. In this book, the head of each tribe summarizes his history and his testament to his tribe. One of the testaments is that of Levi, Jacob's third son, who describes what happened after he took blood vengeance, together with Simon, against Shechem for his act against their sister Dina.

> *As I was tending the flocks in Abel-Maoul a spirit of under-*
> *standing from the Lord came upon me, and I observed all human*
> *beings making their way in life deceitfully. Sin was erecting walls*
> *and injustice was ensconced in towers. I kept grieving over the*
> *race of the sons of men, and I prayed to the Lord that I might be*
> *delivered. Then sleep fell upon me, and I beheld a high mountain,*
> *and I was on it. And behold, the heavens were opened, and an*
> *angel of the Lord spoke to me: "Levi, Levi, enter!" And I entered*
> *the first heaven, and saw there much water suspended. And again*
> *I saw a second heaven much brighter and more lustrous, for there*
> *was a measureless height in it. And I said to the angel, "Why are*
> *these things thus?" And the angel said to me, "Do not be amazed*
> *concerning this, for you shall see another heaven more lustrous and*
> *beyond compare. And when you have mounted there, you shall*
> *stand near the Lord. You shall be his priest and you shall tell forth*
> *His mysteries to men. You shall announce the one who is about to*
> *redeem Israel... Your life shall be from the Lord's provision; He*
> *shall be to you as field and vineyard and produce, as silver and*
> *gold."* (The Testament of Levi, 2:3-10, 12)[13]

Levi, who is cursed at the end of the Book of Genesis, in his dream receives a plot twist in which he is told that he has become the chosen son. Besides the connotation of deep sleep that echoes the story of Adam, the dream has its own unique significance. Instead of being chastised for his act of violence, Levi is rewarded

---

13   English translation: https://www.thefirmament.org/wpcontent/ uploads/pdf/Testaments%20 of%20the%20Patriarchs.pdf

for his actions and virtue, and becomes the High Priest, whose role it is to serve God.

JOSEPH'S DREAMS

The most prominent biblical figure whose name is associated with dreams is Joseph. Joseph, whose brothers nicknamed him "The Dreamer," began dreaming dreams at a young age, solved others' dreams at a later age, and ultimately saw his dreams come to pass. Joseph dreamed two dreams at the beginning.

The first was "For, behold, we were binding sheaves in the field, and, lo, my sheaf arose, and also stood upright; and, behold, your sheaves came round about, and bowed down to my sheaf," (Genesis 37:7) and the second was "Behold, the sun and the moon and eleven stars bowed down to me."(Ibid 37:9)

Despite the similarity between the two dreams, Rabbi Yosef Dov HaLevi Soloveitchik explains in his book *Yemei Zikaron* (Days of Memory) that these are different dreams. The first is an economic dream that deals with power and wealth. In it, Joseph recounts how his sheaf is placed in the center and the rest of the sheaves are bowing down to him. Following the first dream, the word "jealousy" is not mentioned. The brothers react with hatred but not with jealousy: "And they hated him yet the more for his dreams, and for his words." (Ibid., 37:11) In other words, they did not envy him, because the dream contained no vision of his arrogance towards them, but rather hated him. This dream mentioned only the brothers' sheaves, not Jacob or Joseph's mother, Rachel.

The second dream, in contrast, has nothing to do with economics, but rather is a spiritual one. Joseph sees not only the heavenly entities bowing down to him, but his whole family recognizes his spiritual kingship, recognizes the future Messiah son of Joseph, with even his father Jacob bowing down to him. Here jealousy is already mentioned, along with Jacob's response: he reprimands him, but at the same time keeps the dream in mind. The second dream, according to Rabbi Soloveitchick, has not yet come true. Even though his brothers do bow down to him, as in the first dream, the kingship is ultimately given to Yehuda and not to Joseph, who is left with a different role in Jewish history.

Joseph's own dreams are no ordinary dreams. Joseph is revealed not only as a dreamer of dreams but also as someone who knows how to interpret them. Thrown into the pit by his brothers, Joseph is sold to the Ishmaelites and ends up a slave in Potiphar's house. As a result of slander by Potiphar's wife, after she fails in her attempt to entice Joseph into sexual relations with her, Joseph finds himself in prison together with two of Pharaoh's ministers, whose reasons for imprisonment are not specified in the Biblical text.

THE DREAMS OF THE CUP-BEARER AND THE BAKER

Joseph meets Pharaoh's eunuchs one morning, sees that they are "furious," and asks what happened to cause their bad moods. In response, both the cup-bearer and the baker tell him the dreams they had. The cup-bearer dreamed about a vine with three ripe clusters of grapes that he squeezes into a cup and serves to Pharaoh. Joseph explains to him that this is a message in which the three clusters of grapes symbolize three days, after which he will be pardoned and return to his position as the Pharaoh's cup-bearer. The baker, in contrast, dreams of three baskets of bread resting on his head, with a bird eating from the uppermost basket. This time Joseph gives a pessimistic interpretation to the dream, explaining that it, too, is a message, predicting that in three days the baker will be executed and a bird will eat his flesh.

There are noticeable differences between the two dreams. Regarding the cup-bearer, who recounts his dream first, the fact that he is Pharaoh's slave is noted in the text, and his active involvement in the dream is clear, along with the fact that the bunch of grapes is placed before him. In contrast, the baker seems not to have originally intended to share his dream, but only does so to follow the cup-bearer, as he says, "Me, too, in my dream." This indicates that he does not see his own self-worth as justifying telling his dream from the start, but only considers himself worthy of joining with someone else's dream. Moreover, in the dream, the baker behaves passively, not connecting with Pharaoh in any way, and all the action in the dream takes place above his head (rather than in front of him as with the cup-bearer).

Even if these interpretations do not match Joseph's earlier abilities as a dream interpreter, they certainly bolster his reputation, revealing him as "the man of dreams." Joseph's predicted scenarios turn out to be accurate. Three days after the dreams, Pharaoh celebrates his birthday and decides to pardon the cup-bearer. Before the servant leaves the jail, Joseph asks him to remember him, that in exchange for the dream interpretation he recommends to Pharaoh that Joseph be released from jail. The cup-bearer is indeed released, but forgets Joseph and goes back to his regular life until he is reminded later on, when Pharaoh seeks an interpreter for his own dreams. The midrash in Bereishit Rabba (89,3) criticizes Joseph for placing his faith in the cup-bearer and not in God, explaining that due to Joseph's repeated plea to be remembered (repeating the root of the Hebrew word "remember me" twice), two more years were added to Joseph's time in jail before he was finally released.

The cup-bearer's dream is given unexpected significance from another source, when the Jerusalem Talmud explains that the source of drinking four cups of wine at the Passover Seder comes from the four instances of the word "cup" in the cup-bearer's dream. Some see in the cup-bearer's redemption from jail a sign of the Jewish people's future redemption and exodus from slavery to freedom.

PHARAOH'S DREAMS

The Bible tells us that Pharaoh, King of Egypt, dreamed two dreams that left him greatly shaken: "*Vatipa'em rucho*" ("His spirit was troubled"). The Sages compare this verse with a similar one referring to Nebuchadnezzar, King of Babylon, in the Book of Daniel: "*Vatitpaem rucho*" (Daniel 2:1), noting that the Hebrew letter '*tav*' appears only once in the word regarding Pharaoh and twice regarding Nebuchadnezzar. They explain this difference to refer to the dream's effect on the two rulers: Pharaoh remembers his dream, while Nebuchadnezzar's distress leads him to forget the dream's power and its content.

Nachmanides explains another difference between the two dreams, based on the wording of the description of Nebuchadnezzar's dreams compared to Pharoah's:

> *And the meaning of "and Pharaoh awoke, and, behold, it was a*
> *dream" – behold it was a complete dream before him; the language*
> *of Rabbeinu Shlomo. And in my opinion, it is hinting that he*
> *lay in his bed awake, thinking about his dream that perhaps he*
> *would see something more a third time, and when he got up in*
> *the morning and did not dream any more, his spirit was troubled,*
> *and that is the meaning of "And it came to pass in the morning*

that his spirit was troubled," but about Nebuchadnezzar it is said, "And his spirit was troubled and his sleep broke from him" (Daniel 2:1), *because even at night his heart did not rest* (according to Ecclesiastes 2:23). *And the text mentions "Pharaoh awoke" – it is according to the idea mentioned in "The Book of Sleep," that if a person dreams one dream and then after that another dream that is not connected to the first one, then the first one does not come to pass, therefore it is said, that when he awoke from the dream, and thought about it until morning, perhaps he will have a third dream, having already seen two dreams. And lo, Pharaoh himself recognized that they were the same matter, and therefore the text says, "it is a dream," and thus he said "I have dreamed a dream and there is none that can interpret it"* (ibid., 15), *and did not say "dreams," and that is the meaning of "And I saw in my dream"* (ibid., 22) *but the text says "there was none that could interpret them unto Pharaoh"* (ibid., 8), *to say that there was no one to interpret even one of them.*

Nebuchadnezzar does not make a connection between the different dreams he had. In contrast, Pharaoh sees his two dreams as one, even though the text describes two separate dreams.

1. **The first dream:** Pharaoh sees seven thin cows eating seven fat cows.

2. **The second dream:** Pharaoh sees seven withered stalks of grain swallowing seven full, healthy stalks.

When Pharaoh awakens, he is agitated and calls for the wise men (sorcerers) of Egypt to interpret his dream; they try to interpret the two dreams but only in the context of Pharaoh's personal and family life. After the Egyptian wise men repeatedly fail to interpret the dream, the cup-bearer finally remembers Joseph, and Pharaoh decides to bring him out of the jail to come interpret his dreams. Joseph answers Pharaoh that the two dreams are in fact one, with identical meanings. According to the Zohar (1,196), Pharaoh deliberately changed part of the description of the dream to test Joseph, to see if he would indeed manage to describe the dream in its proper order.

The dream is interpreted as a heavenly sign in which God is hinting to Pharaoh of abundance that will lead to years of plenty, followed by years of famine. Even though this interpretation is not mentioned in the dream itself, Joseph proposes storing food during the predicted years of plenty in order to ensure the survival of the Kingdom of Egypt and its people during the years of famine. Midrash Aggadah explains that Joseph's proposal reminds Pharaoh that it indeed matches his dream, and thus he is convinced by Joseph's interpretation, rather than that of his own senior advisors, despite their extensive experience in dream interpretation. Pharaoh marvels at Joseph's wisdom, his young age notwithstanding, and identifies him as someone who carries the "spirit of God." He appoints him as his second-in-command in order to implement his proposal and thus fulfill the dream

BILAAM'S DREAM AND HIS PROPHECY

Bilaam ben Beor is mentioned in the Books of Numbers and Deuteronomy as someone who tried to curse the Jewish people after Balak ben Tzipor, King of Moav, hired his services. The Sages describe Bilaam as one of the seven prophets of the Gentile nations (Baba Batra 15), connecting Bilaam to Laban. According to the

Targum Yonatan, "Laban the Aramean is Bilaam," while in the Talmud, Bilaam is identified as the son of Laban, and in the Zohar (Vayishlach) he is portrayed as Laban's grandson. Like Laban, God also reveals himself to Bilaam at night, and in both cases the content of the dream is a warning. In addition, both figures are described as magicians, wizards, and soothsayers.

On his way to Balak, Bilaam encounters an angel who causes his she-ass to lie down. After Bilaam tries to urge the animal forward by hitting her, she opens her mouth and argues with him: "And the LORD opened the mouth of the ass, and she said unto Balaam: 'What have I done unto thee, that thou hast smitten me these three times?'" (Numbers 22:28) The she-ass's speech is considered so exceptional that in *Ethics of the Fathers* (5:6), it is mentioned as one of the 10 things created on the sixth day of Creation at dusk, a moment before the completion of Creation. Commentators debate both the course of events and how they happened. While Nachmanides states that the miracle was that the she-ass spoke in human language, Maimonides (*Guide for the Perplexed* 2,42) explains that it occurred in a "prophetic vision." Maimonides' position is consistent with what we said above, for he holds that any prophecy or encounter with an angel cannot take place while someone is awake, except in the case of Moses. The words of Maimonides and the Abarbanel (below) also align with many midrashim that describe the appearance of the angel and the encounter with the she-ass as taking place in a dream.

Abarbanel raises many questions about the story of Bilaam and the encounter with the angel and the she-ass, denying the interpretation that the events actually happened as described. Accordingly, he explains that everything that happened to Bilaam was a dream. Via this explanation, Abarbanel resolves Bilaam's suggestion to

Balak's emissaries, "Now therefore, I pray you, tarry ye also here this night, that I may know what the LORD will speak unto me more." (Numbers 22:19) as well as his earlier proposal, "Lodge here this night..." (22:8)

An interesting discovery was made in Tel Deir Alla (Jordan) in 1968, when an inscription was found (catalogued as KAI 312) dated to 840-760 BCE. In the inscription, one can identify an apocalyptic prophecy of Bilaam, beginning with the words "Bilaam ben Beor man who sees God."

GIDEON'S DREAMS

Gideon ben Yoash, from the tribe of Menasseh, was the fifth judge to lead the Jewish people during the Judges Period (12th century BC). Gideon was also called Jerubbaal (1 Samuel, 12:11) and Jerub-besheth (2 Samuel, 11:21). He was known as a leader who came to power after a national crisis. After a long period during which the Israelites suffered from attacks by the Midianites, Amalekites, and other nomadic tribes, they remained enslaved to the Midianites, who ruled over them for seven years. This rule led to the plundering and diminishing of the Israelites' sources of livelihood, as well as a sense of national disgrace. After the people cried out, an angel of God was sent to promise them salvation in the near future. The angel also came to Gideon while he was at work threshing wheat in a wine press (and not on a threshing floor, for fear that the Midianites would impound his crop). The angel blessed Gideon, who responded with criticism of God and His lack of miracles, expressing fear that God had abandoned His watch over the Israelites and left them at the mercy of the Midianites.

The angel did not accept Gideon's words, declaring instead that the judge had the power to save the Jewish people. From reading the plain sense of the text, it seems that it is in fact the rebellious words against God and the daring to hurl a challenge at the angel that indicate the appropriate qualities for leadership. Gideon rejects the angel's words and claims that his young age, as well as his unsuitability, contradict the angel's words about his power to save. The angel encourages Gideon and promises him that God will be with him. Gideon, not satisfied with the angel's promises, demands proof that it is indeed an angel with magic powers. The angel works miracles by sending forth fire that devours meat and matzas even when Gideon dumps soup on them. After seeing these signs, Gideon comes to believe that it is indeed an angel.

Despite what the angel said, Gideon takes his first step towards leadership at night, not during the day. He builds an altar to God and at the same time destroys his father's idol worship – an altar to Baal and a tree dedicated to the goddess Ashera. He avoids a confrontation after a discussion with his father, during which the father suggests that if there were something real in the idol worship, she was the one who had to take vengeance on Gideon and not her servants.

Gideon continues his military campaigns and tries to defeat the Midianites in the Jezreel Valley in a campaign that apparently fails. After that, he prepares to fight the Midianites again, but before that he asks for signs from God. To prove Gideon's victory, God provides signs using a fleece placed on the ground, where one time the fleece is wet and the surrounding ground is dry, and a second time the opposite. After these signs, God instructs Gideon to make do with a minimal martial force in order to prove that God is partner in the campaign and the military victory. After many soldiers are weeded out, Gideon is left with only 300 fighting men.

Gideon is instructed by God to attack at night, but if he is still afraid, God advises him to descend to the Midianite camp together with his servant, listen to their conversations and thus garner confidence. Thus Gideon and the servant set out on a secret nighttime reconnaissance of the Midianite camp. During their expedition, Gideon assesses the state of morale in the enemy camp.

He reaches the edge of the camp at the time of changing of the guard, and listens to two Midianites discussing their dreams. One tells his companion about a dream in which he saw a Midianite tent knocked down by a loaf of barley bread. The other Midianite interprets the dream as signaling the Midianites' future defeat in the battle with Gideon. When Gideon hears both the dream and its interpretation, he understands that the Midianites fear his army, and he formulates a plan to subjugate the enemy by attacking their morale.

One can see how Gideon seeks out signs and wonders before each significant stage of his leadership. Although he demands from the angel and from God that they show supernatural proof, in the military stage, where Gideon would seem most in need of a miracle, his fear dissipates by hearing a dream and its interpretation. Does the dream only reflect the soldiers' low morale? Is the timing of Gideon's hearing of the dream also a supernatural act? One can see how dreams receive significance that leads to changing a national paradigm, to victory, to a change of status in the Land of Israel, and to the end of the Israelites' enslavement.

SAMUEL AND DREAMS

One of the first revelations to appear in a challenging period is one that appears while Samuel, Hanna's son, is staying in God's house, as she had promised when she prayed for a son. The text describes how during that time, "there was no frequent vision" (1 Samuel 3:1), meaning that prophecy and speaking with God were lacking in that period and were not common either in reality or in people's awareness. The text describes Samuel lying in God's temple, where the Lord's ark was located, when God calls to him. At first Samuel is sure that it is Eli the Priest calling him, and he approaches the priest and says "Here I am." Eli explains that it was not he who called him, and sends him back to lie down. Already in this description, one can sense that Samuel's lying down, as well as the fact that "there was no frequent vision" at that time, were the reasons that God spoke to Samuel via a dream. Even after Eli tells Samuel that apparently it is God speaking to him and Samuel answers God, "Speak, your servant is listening," the prophetic revelation still takes place at night. The text describes how Samuel remains lying down "until the morning," which could be interpreted either that he was shaken by the harsh prophecy about the future of Eli's family, or simply that he woke up from his dream in the morning. According to some commentators, the fact that Samuel not only receives revelation in a dream – but also appears to Saul in a dream – in some way brings the prophet full circle regarding dreams.

SAUL AND THE NECROMANCER

In 1 Samuel, Chapter 28, we read of Saul's encounter with the necromancer, who was some kind of witch. As was customary in ancient times, before setting out on a military or political operation, kings would consult with and obtain a blessing from a prophet or priest, to know that they had the blessing of God for what they were about to do. Other famous kings also did this, such as Jehoshaphat and Achav, who asked the prophets before the war with Aram whether indeed they should go. Seeking out God was done, as noted, by inquiring of the prophets, by asking a question using the *Urim and Thummim* (a device from an ancient period that helps receive transmissions from God) that were placed on the High Priest's chest, or by querying a dream.

Before the battle with the Philistines, Saul asks for God's word and refuses to accept the fact that God does not answer him via any spiritual "medium." It is mentioned there that the spiritual media that Samuel tries includes dreams: "And when Saul inquired of the LORD, the LORD answered him not, neither by dreams, nor by Urim, nor by prophets."(1 Samuel 28:6) Instead of inquiring in a dream or of a prophet or via *Urim and Thummim*, in which the king would ask and wait passively for an answer, Saul chooses otherwise. He seeks out a necromancer, even though he himself had banished the necromancers and forbidden querying them as part of his war against idol worship. Due to his declared policy, necromancers worked underground and avoided acting publicly. But given the lack of response via the accepted tools for understanding God's word, Saul disguises himself and seeks to force a spirit of the dead to arise and answer his question: What will happen in the war with the Philistines?

The necromancer raises Samuel, and the Bible describes how Samuel is indeed revealed to Saul and reprimands him for using this practice. "Why hast thou disquieted me, to bring me up?" (1 Samuel 28:15). Saul apologizes and explains that he did it because he lacked any response from God. Samuel still wonders, "Why are you asking me?" while informing him that his kingdom is soon to be torn from him and given to David, and that God is leaving him.

There are various interpretations on what actually happened between Saul and the necromancer, with Biblical commentators and thinkers expressing their positions on magic and rationalism via this discussion. The disagreement appears as early as the Geonic Period (sixth-eleventh century CE) (*Otzar Hageonim l'Hagiga, Response Section*, p. 2). Rabbi Shmuel ben Hafni, one of the Geonim of the Sura Yeshiva, whose position is conveyed by Rabbi David Kimchi, also known as Radak, a French rabbi from the 13th century, stated that it was a "prank" and a trick on the woman's part and not something that actually happened. Maimonides and the Ralbag followed suit, explaining that things did not really happen the way they are described. The Ralbag held that it was an action that influenced the power of imagination, and according to Maimonides and also his son, it was some kind of dream and not a real occurrence.

However, some take the view that things did occur as described. Rabbi Sa'adia Gaon and Rabbi Hai Gaon, in the dispute among the Geonim, took the position that the figure of Samuel did in fact arise and come to life, but that it was not the witch who raised him, but rather that God decided to do so. One can also understand this from the simple meaning of the verses describing Samuel's encounter with God, as well as from Midrash Tanchuma, Parshat Emor. Similar positions appear in *Questions and Answers* (Part 3, Section 642) by Rabbi David ben Zemara (Radbez), the leader of the Jewish community in Egypt and then in Safed five hundred years ago, and the Abarbanel,[14] who claimed that the position of Maimonides and the Ralbag contradicts "the literal text." The Malbim, Rabbi Leibush ben Yehiel Michal, also explains at length how the act of necromancy succeeded:

---

14   Don Isaac Abarbanel (1437-1509) was a rabbi, statesman, and philosopher from a Spanish-Jewish aristocratic family who, among his many positions, also served as Minister of Finance in Portugal, Castile, Aragon, and Naples.

Did not the Sages in their tales tell of the act of necromancy which was still practiced in the days of the Mishnaic and Talmudic sages, and stated that it was within their power to actually raise the dead from their graves, and said that the necromancer saw the dead person and the petitioner heard the voice, and said that if the petitioner was a commoner the dead person would rise head downwards and if he were a king the dead person would rise normally, and all this they were able to say because this craft was known, commonly practiced in their days, and they knew all its aspects.

How could the magic gain power over the prophet's soul?... The exalted soul from above would flee as soon as the man died and return to the God who gave it. But the amorphous spirit that comes into being with the physical body does not flee until the body decays in the grave after 12 months, as it is said, "All the 12 months it rises and falls" (Babylonian Talmud, Shabbat 152b), because it is essentially connected to the body, and as long as no alchemy is done by bonding and refinement, the body will decay and its parts will separate, it is still below and the necromancer has the power to rule over it, and she has the power to predict the future by the magic act, and yet Samuel's upper soul in its glory stands before God in the land of the living, and only the spirit that still clings to the physical body, the necromancer gains control over the spirit to trap it by magic. (Malbim, 1 Samuel, 28)

There are some opinions that even describe the necromancer as a different woman from the image of the witch that comes to mind. In the midrash, the necromancer at Ein Dor is described as the wife of Zefania, mother of Abner. Rabbi Isaac Arama, in his book

Akeidat Yitzhak (The Binding of Isaac) (Chapter 65) writes that one cannot say that Saul, God's anointed, sinned with the necromancer, moreover because he was the one who banished them all, and how could it be that some still remained underground? Therefore, the Akeidat Yitzhak explains that it was a wise woman who had learned how to perform all sorts of spells, and Saul sought her help in order to use her knowledge to discover God's attitude about the battle with the Philistines.

SOLOMON'S DREAM AT GIBEON

King Solomon received kingship over all the Jewish people from his father, David, edging out his brother Absalom who wanted to reign in David's place, as well as his brother Adonyahu, who had already planned his coronation ceremony together with all his brothers except Solomon, and even had the support of Evyatar the Priest and Yoav ben Tzuria, commander of the army. With the help of Nathan the Prophet and Solomon's mother, a quick anointing ceremony was held to crown Solomon as king. At the time, King Solomon was only 12 years old, according to the book *Seder Olam*, which deals with Jewish historical chronology. This is reinforced by Solomon's dialogue in a dream at Gibeon, in which he points out that he lacks experience in leading a large number of people, being only a "young boy."

His rule is established by fulfilling his father's last testament. One of the significant events in establishing his rule appears via a dream that King Solomon has at Gibeon, described in detail in 1 Kings, Chapter 3. After Solomon brings 1,000 sacrifices, God appears to him in a dream and offers to grant him whatever he asks for. Solomon chooses to pass up the material needs that a man is usually expected to request, and instead asks for leadership ability in which he will receive "an understanding heart to judge Thy people, that I may discern between good and evil." (1 Kings 3:9) Solomon's request is granted and he receives wealth and honor alongside a promise that he will merit a long life, as long as he strictly keeps God's commandments. Immediately after the dream, King Solomon's impressive judging ability appears in the famous judgment that he issued in the case of the two women claiming the same child, which grants him state sanction to lead the people.

According to tradition, King Solomon is the author of the Book of Ecclesiastes. In it, he expresses a different attitude about dreams, admonishing "For through the multitude of dreams and vanities there are also many words; but fear thou God." (Eccl. 5:6) He thus advises people to avoid listening to personal dreams or dream interpretations that only distract a person from his path and his purpose.

Besides the famous dream, there is a unique connection with the Song of Songs, in which Solomon also addresses dreams. One can see in the reference "On my bed at night I sought the one I love; I sought him, but did not find him" (Cant. 3:1) and the verse "I sleep but my heart is awake" (Ibid. 5:2), as well as the attempts at encounters in which the text describes the lover arising from sleep and just missing the beloved.

One can see an interesting parallel between the description of Solomon at Gibeon in 1 Kings and the revelation in Chronicles:

1 Kings 3	2 Chronicles 1
5 "In Gibeon the LORD appeared to Solomon in a dream by night; and God said: 'Ask what I shall give thee.'"	7 "In that night did God appear unto Solomon, and said unto him: 'Ask what I shall give thee.'"
15 "And Solomon awoke, and, behold, it was a dream; and he came to Jerusalem, and stood before the ark of the covenant of the LORD, and offered up burnt-offerings, and offered peace-offerings, and made a feast to all his servants."	13 "So Solomon came [from his journey] to the high place that was at Gibeon, from before the tent of meeting, unto Jerusalem; and he reigned over Israel."

Some commentators explain the difference by observing that at that time there was resistance to dreams. In contrast, others interpret the text in Chronicles as lending credence to dreams and showing how the dream was equal in weight to prophecy, since in his dream King Solomon encounters God directly.

PROTECTION AGAINST BAD DREAMS FOR KING SOLOMON

Solomon's soaring via the dream also ends with his increasing fears as he lies down to sleep. The Song of Songs describes how he placed 60 warriors around his bed: "Behold, it is the litter of Solomon; threescore mighty men are about it, of the mighty men of Israel." (Cant. 3:7) Sixty warriors protected him from terrors of the night, and this eventually became a symbol of how one could protect oneself from bad dreams. Thus, for example, Rabbi Moshe Mat, a disciple of Solomon Luria, in his 1591 book, *Mateh Moshe*, writes that Solomon's 60 mighty men were "the Priestly Blessing which contains 60 letters, which were engraved on Solomon's bed against night terrors, and they are a talisman for banishing bad dreams." That is, Solomon's warriors were not actual men, but rather to be understood spiritually, and such protection can be duplicated by reciting Biblical verses that create angels or spiritual forces that protect against those bad dreams. In his book, Rabbi Moshe Mat accords significance to protecting oneself from dreams in his explanation of the various verses said before sleep, explaining how each verse is directed towards protection from and banishing of the harmful, destructive forces that come during the night.

DREAMS AND THE PROPHET JEREMIAH

Jeremiah ben Hilkiyah was a contemporary of the Prophet Ezekiel. Jeremiah prophesied about the Jewish people during the rules of the kings Josiah, Jehoahaz, Jehoiakim, Jehoiachin, and Zedekiah. His prophecies caused him to be hated by the people, by and large, and his enemies called him a "quarrelsome person." The people of his home city of Anatot, including his father's house, opposed his prophecies and forbade him to prophesize until he moved to Jerusalem. Only in the days of Tzidkiyah, who admired Jeremiah as a prophet, did his reputation improve among those around him. According to the Ari,[15] Jeremiah is even buried in Jerusalem in the Guard's Court-yard – the prison in Jerusalem in the First Temple Period.

Even though dreams and prophecy often seem to be inter-changeable, Jeremiah stresses the difference between the two, chal-lenging and criticizing the false prophets who shared their dreams with the public while trying to fool the people:

15 Ari is an acronym for Rabbi Yitzhak ben Shlomo Luria (1572-1534), who was involved in mysti-cism and, although he died at the age of 38, is considered a popular figure among those involved in Jewish mysticism, which includes deciphering divine secrets, influencing reality, and understanding how the world works.

I have heard what the prophets have said, That prophesy lies in My name, saying: "I have dreamed, I have dreamed." How long shall this be? Is it in the heart of the prophets that prophesy lies, And the prophets of the deceit of their own heart? That think to cause My people to forget My name By their dreams which they tell every man to his neighbor, As their fathers forgot My name for Baal. The prophet that hath a dream, let him tell a dream; And he that hath My word; let him speak My word faithfully. What hath the straw to do with the wheat? Saith the LORD. (Jeremiah 23:25-28)

This is not the only time that Jeremiah seeks to reject dreams and their significance. The increasing use of dreams and the connection between false prophets and dreams is repeated in other places: "But as for you, hearken ye not to your prophets, nor to your diviners, nor to your dreams, nor to your soothsayers, nor to your sorcerers, that speak unto you, saying: 'Ye shall not serve the king of Babylon' (27:9) and also: 'For thus saith the LORD of hosts, the God of Israel: Let not your prophets that are in the midst of you, and your diviners, beguile you, neither hear- ken ye to your dreams which ye cause to be dreamed.'" (29:8)

The matter of dreams and Jeremiah's rebuke did not remain mere facts from the past. Maimonides, in *The Laws which are the Foundations of the Torah* (10,3), writes about prophecy and states parameters by which one can use clear criteria to distinguish between a true prophet and a false one. He notes the words of the Prophet Jeremiah in order to distinguish between a prophet, whose every word comes to pass, and someone recounting his dream, whose words are like a mixture of straw and grain, and will not fully come to pass.

THE PERSONALITY OF DANIEL, THE "MASTER OF DREAMS"

Another figure whose story parallels that of Joseph, not only in the matter of dreams, is Daniel. Here are a number of parallels between the two stories:

1. Like Joseph, Daniel did not grow up in his natural place, when Nebuchadnezzar's minister Ashpenaz took him as part of a group of gifted children (including Hananiyah, Misha'el and Azariyah) to serve the king.

2. Daniel, like Joseph, dreams dreams, some of which come true and others are prophecy for the future.

3. Both men have additional foreign names. While Joseph was called Zaphnath-Paaneah, Daniel was called Belteshazzar – "guards the king's life."

4. Like Joseph, who successfully overcame temptation with Potiphar's wife, Daniel overcame the temptation to eat forbidden foods.

5. Daniel and Joseph were both "thrown into a pit;" Joseph faced snakes and scorpions (Shabbat 22), while Daniel faced lions.

6. Both of them are described as "good-looking" (Genesis 39:6, Daniel 1:4) and "wise" (Genesis 41:39, Daniel 1:4).

7. In both stories, following the kings' dreams, there is
    first a consultation with the sorcerers; then there is a
    recommendation by an external source that the king
    should consult with the Jewish hero as an interpreter of
    dreams. The hero then interprets the dreams, adding a
    practical recommendation (for Pharaoh, storing food;
    for Nebuchadnezzar, giving charity), and finally rises to
    greatness following his interpretation of the dreams and
    is dressed in royal garments. Both stories also feature the
    hero's clear Jewish identity, their urgent summons to the
    king to interpret the dreams, the dreams' awe-inspiring
    effects on the two kings, and others.

Daniel is accorded a position of honor, "Chief of the Sorcerers"
(Daniel 4:9) after he interprets the dreams of Nebuchadnezzar, who
remembers not only the interpretation of the dream but also what
he dreamed. His interpretations are revealed to be true, and after
the interpretation of the dream that featured the idol, the King of
Babylon even asks to bring Daniel an offering as though he were
a god. After Nebuchadnezzar's death, however, Daniel's reputation
fades, to the point where there is an opinion that "Hatach" in the
story of Esther is Daniel and he is named thus because "*hatachuhu
m'gdulato*" ("he was cut off from his greatness"). But a riddle written on the wall of Belshazzar's palace – which Daniel interprets
correctly – leads to his reappointment to a court position, with the
third highest rank in the Babylonian Kingdom.

In the Persian court, people jealous of his practices and his
position plot against him, leading him to be thrown into the lions'

den. However, the lions do not harm him, and this news is widely publicized, boosting the reputations of both Daniel and the God of Israel. The Talmud (Yoma 77) describes Daniel as someone who, if placed on one side of a scale, would weigh more than all the wise men of all the nations.

Daniel's personality, like his dreams, leave a stamp of ambiguity. In the Book of Daniel, it is unclear whether he was a prophet or merely a visionary. Several interpretations of his standing have been suggested: some place him in the rank of a mid-level prophet (Maimonides), others hold that he was some kind of visionary but not a prophet (Nachmanides, Rabbi Judah Halevi, Ibn Ezra), or that he was a prophet but not sent to Israel to speak his prophecies (Rashi, Maharsha), or that he was a different type of prophet, i.e., who did not rebuke and chastise the people with his prophecies but only stirred them (Tosefot Harosh).

A unique position is taken by Rabbi Aryeh Leib Ginsberg, known for two books that have become centerpieces of the Jewish library: *Sha'agat Aryeh* (Roar of the Lion) and *Turei Even*. (Columns of Stone). According to the approach in *Turei Even*, Daniel's revelations were not via prophecy but via dreams:

> From his [Rashi's] commentary, the meaning is that he was a prophet, but did not prophesy for others. The words themselves do not convey this, but that he was not a prophet at all, and the words of the mighty God never came to him, and all the prophecies about the future in the Book of Daniel were by an angel or dream, as is explained in the Scripture.
>
> (Turei Even, Tractate Megillah 3)

Jeremiah's words about false prophets trickled down through the generations and were even fixed in Jewish law. A number of famous rabbis and adjudicators of Jewish law have stated that anyone who has a dream in which he is commanded to negate commandments from the Torah – or even from the Oral Law – is forbidden to obey this dream and should not pay attention to it at all.

NEBUCHADNEZZAR'S DREAMS

Two significant dreams of Nebuchadnezzar are described in the Book of Daniel:

1.   **Nebuchadnezzar's dream about the statue** (Daniel 2:29-46) Nebuchadnezzar has a dream that will not let him rest, so he asks the Babylonian magicians to guess the dream and its interpretation. Failed attempts by the magicians lead him to order a death sentence for all those who tried to guess and failed. This order makes waves both inside and outside the palace, and Daniel decides to try to help. At first Daniel prays to God to reveal to him the dream and its interpretation. His prayer is answered, which causes Daniel to approach Arioch, the man in charge of executing the failed magicians, and asks to be brought to the king so he can offer the interpretation of the dream. First of all, Daniel correctly guesses the dream itself – the "Statue Dream" – and Nebuchadnezzar confirms that it was indeed the dream that he saw. After that, Nebuchadnezzar asks for the interpretation and Daniel explains it to him.

     Nebuchadnezzar's dream takes place at the beginning of the Period of Kingdoms, immediately following the destruction of the Temple and of Israel, which is a significant turning point in world history and for the

Jewish people. Nebuchadnezzar's dream is called the "Statue Dream," since a giant statue appears in it, with its body parts divided according to various types of metal alloys:

- Head of the statue – made of gold
- Chest and arms – silver
- Abdomen and hips – copper
- Thighs – iron
- Soles of the feet – some clay and some iron

After Nebuchadnezzar sees the statue, a large rock appears and crushes the statue to shards as it turns the stone into a mountain. In interpreting the dream, Daniel explains that these are symbols for different kingdoms, and there is a dispute among Bible commentators as to the identity of each kingdom and its relationship to the relevant metal alloy. The stone is the Kingdom of the God of Israel who will rule for eternity, even after the reigns of the other kingdoms have faded away.

2. **Nebuchadnezzar's dream about the tree** (Daniel 4:1-24)
   Nebuchadnezzar's other dream that has an impact in the Book of Daniel is the "tree dream." Here, too, no one can be found to interpret it until Daniel arrives, having already gained recognition as someone who possesses "the spirit of the holy gods." In this dream, the king sees a tree laden with fruit, whose shade and branches grant life to all creatures. This ideal image, however, is rudely cut off by an angel who comes down from Heaven and orders that the tree be cut down, while avoiding uprooting the roots.

The same angel states that the king is destined to live as an animal, imprisoned in iron chains, for a period of seven years/eras.

Daniel once again succeeds in interpreting the dream, explaining that Nebuchadnezzar is fated to be cut off from the kingdom and all his duties. Twelve months after the dream, as Nebuchadnezzar is boasting about his kingdom, the dream comes true and, just as he dreamed, a heavenly voice speaks and Nebuchadnezzar is obliged to flee and to live as a wild beast.

JOB'S DREAM

Job is a unique figure in the Bible; his story deals with a dialogue between him and his friends, as well as between him and God, concerning good and evil, reward and punishment. Job's three friends – Elifaz the Temanite, Bildad the Shuhite, and Zophar the Naamathite – try to comfort him for after hearing of all the misfortunes that have befallen him, attempting to offer an explanation. The friends talk with Job and respond to his questions. Another friend is Elihu, son of Barachel the Buzite, who speaks out after being disappointed with the answers he heard from the other friends.

Dreams appear several times in the Book of Job. One time is in the speech of Elihu, son of Barachel the Buzite, one of Job's friends who chastised him for thinking of himself as a righteous man. After a period of silence, and out of a sense of his own young age and respect for the friends who are older than he is, Elihu decides to speak out, even though Job does not address him. Elihu makes four significant speeches, dealing with God's justice, suffering, people's actions, and more. In the first speech, Elihu speaks about the means of God's revelation, which can come through injuring a person and thus rousing him, or by "revelation in a dream."

Elifaz the Temanite, who appears earlier in the book and is considered the most significant of Job's three friends, also addresses dreams. All his words are based on a vision that came to him "secretly" and a mysterious voice that he heard. During this vision, which some understand as a sort of dream, Elifaz develops his theory that every man sins and therefore he must explain to Job that apparently he also sinned. At any rate, anyone who is suffering must review his deeds and find where he has sinned and is at fault for his suffering. Regarding the voices, the text does not state unequivocally whether Elifaz indeed heard the Holy Spirit or whether it was a kind of dream.

The range of opinions among the Sages regarding Job's identity only confirms the mysteriousness surrounding this figure. Except for the "one of the Rabbis" from Rabbi Shmuel bar Nachmani's yeshiva, who claimed that "Job never existed, but was only a parable," various opinions in the Talmud in Tractate Baba Batra (15) locate Job's identity and that of his generation across an extremely broad time spectrum:

1. **Bar Kappara says:** Job lived in Abraham's time.

2. **Some say:** Job lived in Jacob's time and married Dina, Jacob's daughter.

3. **R. Levi bar Hama says:** Job lived in Moses' time.

4. **Raba says:** He lived in the time of the spies.

5. **R. Natan says:** Job lived during the Kingdom of Sheba.

6. **The Sages say:** Job lived in the days of Kasdim.

7. **Rabbi Yehoshua ben Karcha says:** Job lived in the time of Ahasuerus.

8. **Rabbi Yohanan** and **Rabbi Eliezer say:** Job was one of those who returned to Israel from the Babylonian exile and studied Torah in Tiberias

From a historical point of view, it should be noted that there are two other approaches in the tradition. One is in the Jerusalem Talmud (Sotah, 5:6) and holds that Job was one of Pharaoh's servants and one of the most powerful members of his entourage. The other is the approach of Maimonides in his *Guide for the Perplexed* (3,23), where it is written that Job lived in the time of King David.

Another significant dispute regarding Job is his status and his interface with prophecy. The Talmud is of the opinion that Job was one of the seven prophets who belonged to the Gentile nations, a category whose only other members are Bilaam, Job's father, his three friends, and Elihu, son of Barachel the Buzite. Job's status as a prophet is reinforced by the fact that God reveals Himself to him, which fits the Book of Numbers (12:6): "I will speak with him in a dream." And indeed, Job describes a sort of dialogue that he holds with God, specifically in a dream.

> *For God speaketh in one way, yea in two, though man perceiveth it not. In a dream, in a vision of the night, when deep sleep falleth upon men, In slumberings upon the bed; Then He openeth*

the ears of men, and by their chastisement sealeth the decree.
(Job 33:14-16)

The dialogue he holds via the dream allows us to glimpse the divine revelation that occurs outside a person's familiar environment. The dream and the night vision enable an encounter between the soul and the divine appearance. The use of the word *tardema* (deep sleep) – that echoes the story of Adam – highlights how Job's view of dreams differs from Adam's story, in that Job's experience does not necessarily involve preparation of the dreamer to receive the vision; instead, it comes as a total surprise.

The Babylonian Talmud (Brachot 57a and b) brings various interpretations of the symbols that appear in dreams. The Talmud's list of categories of different things that can appear in dreams, each divided into threes, includes seeing books in one's dream:

*The Rabbis taught: "There are three kings: one who sees David
in a dream – can expect mercies; Solomon – can expect wisdom;
Ahab – should beware of calamities; There are three prophets: one
who sees the Book of Kings – can expect greatness; Ezekiel – can
expect wisdom; Isaiah – can expect consolation; Jeremiah – should
beware of calamities; There are three major scriptures: one who
sees the Book of Psalms – can expect mercies; Proverbs – can expect
wisdom; Job – should beware of calamities; There are three minor
scriptures: one who sees the Song of Songs in a dream – can expect
mercies; Ecclesiastes – can expect wisdom; Lamentations – should
beware of calamities; one who sees the Book of Esther – a miracle
will be performed for him. There are three sages: one who sees
Rabbi in a dream – can expect wisdom; Rabbi Eleazar ben*

Azariyah – can expect riches; Rabbi Yishma'el ben Elisha – should beware of calamities; There are three Torah scholars: one who sees Ben Azariyah in a dream – can expect mercies; Ben Zoma – can expect wisdom; Acher – should beware of calamities."

One can see that there are parallels, which should be considered to be equivalents, even when they appear with different figures or symbols. The connections between things can easily be seen in the table.

Type of dream	Expect mercies	Expect wisdom	Beware of calamities
Kings	David	Solomon	Ahab
Prophets	——-	Ezekiel	Jeremiah
Major scriptures	Psalms	Proverbs	Job
Minor scriptures	Song of Songs	Ecclesiastes	Lamentations
Sages	Rabbi	———-	Rabbi Yishmael ben Elisha
Torah scholars	Ben Azai	Ben Zoma	Acher

One can see unique parallels and connections between the different figures. Despite the disputes over Job's righteousness and when he lived, one thing is not subject to dispute: the book's connection to calamities. The Talmud does not specify whether the person dreaming sees the book or the figure of Job himself, since it is written, "one who sees the Book of Psalms," etc., which seems to mean seeing the book in its entirety; still, there is no clear description of what the person sees in the dream. No one knows what the kings and prophets looked like in real life, so it is the dreamer's subjective interpretation that attributes a figure in a dream to a specific character.

6

THE SECRET OF DREAMS –
MYSTICISM AND DREAMS

The Jews' "Book of Books" provides inspiration and an inexhaustible treasure trove of unique characters, images, and figures of speech, along the way creating a marvelous mosaic of varied references to dreams. Dreams in Jewish texts, however, do not remain just stories. As in other ancient cultures, the Jews saw dreams as having the power to deal with things from beyond. The capacity to dream provides a key to hidden doors that Jewish mysticism and kabbalah saw as a means of rising above our dull, daily reality. While in the past there were prophets who communicated with God and brought His word, we retain a dim connection to that revelation in those dreamers and dreams that are alive and with us, perhaps even in one of you – the readers.

DREAMS AS AN OPENING TO ANOTHER WORLD

Beyond the various Biblical verses showing how humans can communicate with God via dreams, biblical commentaries indicate the unique power of dreams. The Talmud, in Tractate Hagiga (5), states:

And I will surely hide My face on that day, Rabba said. The Holy
One, Blessed be He, said "Even though I hid My face from them, I
will speak with him in a dream."

That is, even though prophecy ended with the destruction
of the Temple and God's distancing Himself from His people,
there is still a unique connection that is expressed in dreams.
As in prophecy, dreams enable access to hidden knowledge from
a heavenly source and the breaking through of accepted limitations that are in place while a person is awake. Accordingly, as we
noted, the Sages claim that a dream is one-sixtieth of prophecy. In
this sentence of the Talmud, we get a glimpse of the importance
of dreams in Judaism in general, and in particular for those who
choose to follow the Jewish kabbalah (kabbalists), who dedicate a
significant part of their lives to self-cleansing, purity, and receiving
inspiration that is close to prophecy.

Dreams are one possible tool for achieving a nullification of
the material world that is closest to death, for during sleep – except
for the brain and the heart – the body and its various needs are
stilled. Over the years, it was said of many kabbalists that they
reached their achievements during sleep and dreaming. The fact
that a large portion of the kabbalah is dedicated to symbols and
interpretations lends power to the symbols appearing in dreams, as
well as the interpretations that one can give them, if the kabbalist
who is dreaming succeeds in refining and purifying himself.

In dreams, the foundations that compose reality are broken
down and then reassembled. Thus new worlds are created, in which
the dreamer can free himself from the bonds of reality and create
new things. It is actually the uncertainty surrounding dreams, along
with the mystery cloaking them, that enables the dream to contain

things that during wakefulness might not be accepted. The Zohar (in Parshat Vayeshev) observes that a dream serves as a sort of prologue, an introduction to things that will occur in the future. According to the Zohar, "You have nothing in the world that until it comes into the world is not dependent on a dream." (Zohar, Parshat Vayeshev) That is, a dream serves as a preface that enables the person to contain and confront a new reality, plot twists in one's life, etc.

CHARACTER AND TIMING OF DREAMS IN KABBALAH

Now we will focus on dreams as they are discussed in the Zohar, the main book of kabbalist teachings, ascribed to the sermons of Rabbi Shimon bar Yochai from the second century CE.

Kabbalistic mysticism, as will be described below, distinguishes among various types of dreams as well as the timing of dreams. There is a significant difference between a daydream and a dream that appears at night, and the hour during the night when a dream appears is also important. One must also take into account what happened during the person's waking hours preceding the dream. In the kabbalah, it is customary to divide the nighttime into two parts. The first is when harmful and destructive forces, belonging to the quality of strict justice, are active. In this part, kabbalists customarily sleep until they get up for *tikkun hatzot* (special prayers said at midnight), at which time the second part of the night comes under the influence of the quality of mercy.

A little math before we begin:

According to the kabbalah, the night is divided into two unequal parts. One part is defined as the time when the quality of strict justice prevails – a phrase indicating that one must be careful during that time. This part comprises the first third of the night, called the first watch. In the second part of the night, which includes the second and third watches, the quality of loving-kindness prevails.

Accordingly, dreams that occur during the first third of the night mostly belong to the imagination, the part influenced by a person's behavior while awake. Thus, according to kabbalah, in the first third, thoughts, fears, worries, and stress break into dreams and influence them, and these are considered to be meaningless dreams. Since there is no reason to ascribe importance to them or to try to provide interpretations for them, it is better to ignore them and see them as a sort of "emptying out" of one's thoughts, without any additional meaning.

In contrast, there are dreams that are connected to levels of holiness, connected to prophecy and to the Holy Spirit. These are described widely in the Zohar and in kabbalists' writings, and there is significance to the symbols appearing in them and to the time when the dream occurs. The Ramchal states that unique dreams are usually those that appear in the third and last portions of the night, as well as Friday night and Sabbath afternoon.

DREAMS IN THE ZOHAR
Dreams as an Interface with a Heavenly World

Statements in various places in the Zohar indicate a concept of dreams as the main interface for receiving heavenly signs. Due to their elevated status, dreams constitute a type of revelation to the soul that comes from the world of the angels (1, 183). In Parshat Vayeshev, the Zohar explains that God announces the coming of everything that enters the world via the Sages. While in the past, this revelation was done through prophecy, today, after the cessation of prophecy, the revelation takes place by dreams or via "birds of heaven."

The soul's attempt to rise during sleep does not always succeed. *Midrash Tehillim* notes (Psalm 11, 6) that when a person sleeps, his soul leaves and wanders the world, and the dreams are part of this wandering. Regarding this wandering, the Zohar clarifies, (Vayikra, 25) in Rashbi's name, that there are demons who, during sleep, prevent the soul from ascending to the upper worlds, and that these worlds are arranged into three levels: upper, middle, and lower. At the lower level, the demons play with the person's soul and frighten it for no reason. The middle level, in contrast, contains mixtures of truth and falsehood, while at the upper level there are true dreams that the demons try to hinder but are unable to contaminate with falsehoods.

Two Kinds of Dreams

The angel appointed to be responsible for dreams is Gabriel, who is mentioned as interpreting the vision in the Book of Daniel (8, 16). According to the Zohar, however, there are two types of dreams, distinguished by which angel is responsible for them. One type is under the responsibility of the angel Michael, and the other the angel Gabriel. The Zohar holds that some dreams come true without any idle elements mixed into them, and these dreams are revealed to the "worthy" (Parshat Miketz). These dreams come true, but without a defined time frame, and may even come true long after they are dreamed. In contrast, dreams intermixed with idle elements come true in a relatively short time, but only the true part of them is realized. The Zohar in Parshat Hayei Sarah notes another feature of such dreams: sometimes the dreams themselves are true, but afterwards they are "infected" by external forces and intermixed with idle elements.

An echo to both kinds of dreams appears in the Zohar (1, 194,1), which explains why Pharaoh dreamed two similar dreams and that one dream was not enough. The Zohar explains that one of Pharaoh's dreams was brought by the angel Michael (the dream about the cows), while the other was by the angel Gabriel (the dream about the sheaves).

The Zohar asserts, "Blessed are the righteous to whom God reveals His secrets in a dream." (Zohar 1, 83a) The righteous who work on their body and spirit can purify their sleep and get the most out of it. The righteous also have dreams of various ranks, and each one is different. The Zohar (Bereishit 199b) explains the verse in Ecclesiastes (5:2), "For a dream cometh through a multitude of business; And a fool's voice through a multitude of words" such that there are several entities responsible for dreams, according to the dreamer's spiritual level. During sleep, a person's soul ascends and visits various places. The place visited and the exposure to unique things depends on the dreamer's level. As we have said, some dreams contain only truth, some are mixed with falsehoods, and some are only falsehoods. The amount of revelation, as well as the amount of damage caused by external angels, depends on the dreamer's level. *Otzar Midrashim* (Hekhalot) expands on what is written in the Zohar:

> *Under this elevated spirit, in this palace there is also an impure*
> *spirit, and its name is "Sartiya." And how many thousands of*
> *angels of destruction are under it, and they are ready at the time*
> *when the dream descends from the holy side – this spirit together*
> *with all the angels of destruction descends with this dream, and*

> *they all intermix with it, and inform that person of mocking*
> *things together with the righteous dream!"*

The Zohar (Raya m'himna, Bamidbar 234b) explains that the dream that comes via an angel is like one-sixtieth of prophecy, compared to a dream that comes via a demon, which is a false dream from the side of death. Similarly, in Parshat Miketz, the Zohar states that there are false dreams and dreams that are true, and if someone is worthy, only true dreams and no false dreams will be revealed to him.

The Zohar's influence can be found in the writings of kabbalistic rabbis such as the Vilna Gaon (known by the acronym The Gra). The Gra observes that the word for dream, *halom*, comes from *halon*, (window). During sleep, a person's soul is released and it rises to the "Heavenly Academy," where it hears sublime things. Rabbi Tzadok Hacohen of Lublin, who wrote a book entitled *Divrei Halomot*, adds that a person should be strict about saying *Hamepil* (a blessing said every night before going to sleep), because without this blessing, a different soul might return to his body while he is asleep. The possibility that a soul might err in navigating its way back to the body indicates a distinction between the dreaming person, the dream, and the soul. That is, dreams are not part of the soul but another facet of the person's personality.

THE NEED FOR SLEEP IN ORDER TO DREAM

In kabbalistic literature, the body is described as standing in a certain opposition to a person's spirituality, which is expressed in the spirit and the soul. Rabbi Menashe ben Yisrael (1604-1657) was a philosopher and kabbalist who was known as the founder of the first Jewish printing house in Amsterdam (one of his most famous students was the philosopher Baruch Spinoza). Thanks to his political activity on behalf of Diaspora Jews, after his death, Jews in England were granted freedom of worship, ultimately leading to the reestablishment of the Jewish community there.

Despite his extensive activism, he found the time to write two works, one of which is *Nishmat Haim*. In this book, Rabbi Menashe ben Yisrael explains why dreams come during sleep and not while someone is awake:

> *It is known that when the material powers are weakened, the intellectual [powers] are strengthened and, as experience has shown, in old age, when a person's strength is already weakened and he does not chase after material desires, he comes closer to wisdom and understanding, and his purpose of serving God ... and since a dream is part of prophecy, just as prophecy does not come to a person until he has nullified his bodily forces and he becomes wise, and this happens during sleep, when the power of the wise spirit increases and the bodily forces are nullified, so dreams do not come during waking hours when the bodily forces are strong, but rather come during sleep which is the time of nullification of the sensations and the material forces, for sleep is one-sixtieth of death.* (Nishmat Haim, Article 3, Chapter 5)

Rabbi Menashe sees a direct connection between being awake, when material needs are felt, and a lack of ability to interface with spiritual forces. Accordingly, the body must be nullified as much as possible, something that happens in old age, during sleep, and at death. Via this approach, Rabbi Menashe explains why the Patriarchs in the Bible gave blessings particularly on their deathbeds. The weakening of the body helps to purify the spiritual forces and thus they sought to bless others. Later in his work, he divides dreams into three levels: prophetic dreams, dreams of divine providence, and natural dreams.

Rabbi Menashe ben Yisrael saw an additional value in dreams, as he was the one to publish *Sefer Ha'achlama*, a book on dreams by the rabbi, physician, and poet Shlomo Elmoli, divided into theoretical, practical, and halachic sections.

SUMMONING A DEAD SOUL IN A DREAM

Encounters with dead people via dreams appear as early as the Tosefta (2nd century CE) in Tractate Shabbat (6,7), where the rabbis write that one of the practices of the Amorites was to kiss a dead person's coffin in order to see him at night. Midrash Kohelet Rabba (9,10) also features many stories of students who underwent purification fasts in order to see Rabbi Hiya in their dreams. Necromancy was forbidden in the Babylonian Talmud (Sanhedrin 65) and anchored in Halacha, when it was ruled by halachic consensus to prohibit the use of these mystical practices. However, despite the clarity of the prohibition, halachic authorities began unravelling it relatively early on. *Sefer Yere'im* (Section 334) states that if anyone makes a sick person swear to return after his death and answer the petitioner's questions, this is not considered "querying of the dead" but rather querying the person's spirit, and that the prohibition is in fact on querying via magic such as a necromancer does:

> One who makes a sick person swear to return after death and tell
> him what he will ask him, this is not querying of the dead, since
> querying of the dead is interpreted as querying of a dead body and
> speaking via magic such as a necromancer, but the necromancer
> raises him from his grave and queries of him in his grave while

someone querying of his spirit this is not querying [of the dead]

since the spirit is not called dead. (Yere'im, Section 334)

This "friendly" practice is also mentioned in *Sefer Hasidim*:

If two people who were good in their lives swore or made a pact
together that if one of them dies, he will inform his friend how
it is in that world, either in a dream or awake. If in a dream the
spirit will come and whisper in the living person's ears or in his
brain like a dreamer, and if they swore that he would speak with
him awake, the dead person will ask an angel to clothe him in an
image of a figure and the scattered spirit will be glued together
until he says to his friend what they made a pact between them
that he would inform him. (Sefer Hasidim, Section 728)

Besides *Ha'yere'im* and *Sefer Hasidim*, other adjudicators of
Jewish law also go in this direction, such as, Rabbi Recanati,[16] and
others. The *Shulchan Aruch*[17] (*Yoreh Deah* 179:14-15) states that this
is permissible, but notes that there are those who permit making
the oath even after the person's death – that is, to make an oath
not with the dead person's body but with his spirit. Already in *Sefer
Hasidim*, and in other writings of Rabbi Yehuda Hehasid, there are
descriptions of all sorts of techniques for summoning dead people
in a dream.

In books of "practical kabbalah," they often choose to use the
magic power of swearing by the holy names in order to cause the
dead to appear in dreams. Via letter combinations and amulets,
those who so wish can summon the dead to appear in their dreams

16   Rabbi Menachem Recanati (1250-1310) was an Italian rabbi and philosopher who wrote a com-
     mentary on the Torah.
17   Jewish religious halachic law book.

and reveal whatever they desire. These techniques appear in official and unofficial writings of practical kabbalah, such as books found in *genizas[18]* from the fourteenth and fifteenth centuries, including the book *Etz Hada'at* by Elisha ben Gad of Ancona in Safed, and *Sefer Harazim*, *Sefer Harba de-Moshe*, *Ma'agal Tov*, *Pinkas Kabbalah Ma'asit*, and *Sefer Hape'ulot* by Rabbi Haim Vital, and more.

These books offer meticulously precise guidance on how to summon the dead; sometimes the person trying to generate such an encounter in a dream must sleep in a cemetery. The books often suggest that, in addition to saying the holy names and specific combinations of letters, one must also bring objects connected to the dead person in order to complete the technical-mystical act of conversing with the dead person in a dream.

It should be noted that more recent kabbalists have avoided using practical kabbalah, in accordance with the Ari's teachings. These include, for example, Rabbi Sdei Hemed, Rabbi Yakov Sapir, Heichal Beracha, Rabbi Yakov Hillel (head of the kabbalistic yeshiva in Jerusalem), and others. Often rabbis and kabbalists follow the position as seen in *Sefer Habrit*, written by Rabbi Pinchas Eliyahu Horovitz in 1797 and distributed throughout Europe and Israel. According to *Sefer Habrit*, all means of causing the dead to take an oath were intentionally concealed by the *Rishonim* (leading rabbis and legal authorities from the 11th to 15th century), and therefore any such instructions to be found, whether in manuscript or in published books, are almost completely garbled and therefore worthless and ineffective. According to Rabbi Horovitz, some of these were deliberately garbled so that they would not be used, such *Sefer Brit Menucha* and *Sefer Raziel*.

---

18   The location where the document collection is saved is old.

THE ARI AND DREAMS

The Ari (the Lion) is the name commonly used to refer to Rabbi Isaac Luria, who conceived and invented a new method in kabbalah, which is connected to the occult. Although he died at the young age of 38, he managed to leave a significant mark on the world of kabbalah, with his paradigm being diametrically opposed to what was accepted at the time. While the kabbalistic understanding saw the Creation as an act of perfection that humanity must strive to return to by correcting their deeds, for the Ari, reality began in fact with the "shattering of the vessels." This shattering was a kind of damage that has prevented the world from receiving the divine light, and the role of humanity is to build the vessels in order to contain that divine light again. Since the Ari wrote down very little, his teachings on kabbalah were mainly publicized by his students and followers.

Dreams were woven into the Ari's life from even before he was born when, according to legend, Elijah the Prophet announced to his father that he would have a son who would illuminate the world. After this, as he grew up and as he began to ascend in holiness and study diligently, he also put harsh restrictions on himself. Following a dream in which it was explained to him that his deeds were not enough, he decided to go to Egypt and enter the "Orchard of Kabbalah."

In his dreams, the Ari saw the direct continuation of his practical actions during waking hours, while taking advantage of the opportunity to quiet the body.

Always when I sleep, my soul rises along paths and ways that are known to me, and the ministering angels bring my soul before Metatron, Sar Hapanim (Angel of the Divine Countenance), and

he asks me to what yeshiva do I want to go, and at that yeshiva
they give me secrets and enigmas and hidden things of the Torah
which have never been heard or known even in the time of the
Tannaim. (Toldot Ha'Ari, 164)

A similar version is found in the writings of Rabbi Avraham
Ha-levi, the Ari's student, who would see the Ari murmuring in
his dream and try to hear what he was saying. When he awoke, he
asked him why he was murmuring; the Ari answered that every
time he slept, there was an angel that welcomed his soul, and asked
where he wanted to go. To the yeshiva of Rabbi Shimon? To the
yeshiva of Rabbi Meir Ba'al Haness? Of Rabbi Akiva? Of Yohanan
ben Zakkai?… Each time a different yeshiva.

Before his death, the Ari warned his students not to read his
writings "because they were not yet complete and God forbid they
should come to cut them short. And if the generation merits it, that
he should come and teach them… in a dream or awake or by any
other means."

RABBI HAIM VITAL AND THE SEFER HACHIZYONOT

Rabbi Haim Vital (1542-1620) studied Halacha in the study hall
of Rabbi Moshe Alshich, and kabbalah in the study hall of Rabbi
Moshe Cordovero together with the Ari; after Rabbi Cordovero's
death, he accepted the Ari as his rabbi. He was considered one of
the senior students of the Ari, and was not only his quintessential
student but also edited, and after the Ari's death, wrote many books
that were later attributed to the Ari. Cordovero had also headed
a group of kabbalists who developed the Ari's philosophy. Rabbi
Haim Vital's famous works include *Etz Haim, Otzrot Haim, Sha'arei*
K'dushah, Sefer haGilgulim, and others.

Besides his Torah writings, there is an additional work, both mystical and autobiographical, in which Rabbi Haim Vital writes down, beginning in 1608, the visions that came to him, alongside his personal dreams, as well as dreams other people had about him. The book indicates dates and is structured like a sort of personal journal. It should be noted that the book was not given a title by Rabbi Vital himself, but by his grandson Moshe Vital, and was eventually published by Chaim Yosef David Azulai in the book *Shem Hag'dolim*. The book was hidden for 350 years before it was finally published.

The book *Sefer Hahizyonot* (Book of Visions) is divided into three sections. The first is an autobiographical journal in which Rabbi Vital records the events he experienced throughout his life, from age 2 to age 70. The second is a description of his own dreams, and the third is a description of dreams that others dreamed about him. The researchers Yosef Avivi and Shifra Assouline disagree as to the connection between the different sections. Here, we will look only at the parts on dreams. He recorded his dreams between 1562-1613, with the most significant dreams usually occurring on Sabbath eves, during the intermediate days of the Sukkot and Passover festivals, and the days of Rosh Hodesh (the New Moon). In these dreams, one can see how Rabbi Vital deals with the expectation of redemption and holds a dialogue with higher powers.

The figures appearing in the dreams vary, including Rabbi Vital himself, who sometimes takes an active part in the dream. There are rabbis and opponents such as Rabbi Yakov Abulafia, who opposed Vital's presenting himself as the Ari's only student, Rabbi Yisrael Najara (author of the famous song *Yah Ribon*), and Rabbi Joseph Ibn Tabul. Biblical figures also appear, as well as dictums regarding the Damascus community, which opposed Rabbi Vital. Throughout the book, it is noted how the spirit reprimands Rabbi Abulafia and the Damascus community describing the community's sinful acts and naming all those who were committing sins.

As we noted, the book describes not only Rabbi Vital's own dreams but also others' dreams about him. Some of the dreams belong to his sons, Shmuel and Yossi. The dreams of Rabbi Vital's sons are not always described in detail, sometimes containing only one biographical fact such as "My son Yossi dreamed that he saw me in the company of a large crowd" (3, 368), or "My son Shmuel dreamed that I sent him to my daughter to buy me cucumbers" (3, 69). In contrast, there are dreams in which Rabbi Vital's sons dream that he is being proclaimed "King of Israel," or that the Messiah comes and they are walking together with their father. The fact that Rabbi Vital accords such meaning even to insignificant dreams and puts them down in writing shows how significant dreams are in the mystical teachings. Mysticism sees life in this world as having the capacity to mingle with higher worlds and other forces, with the interface and encounter occurring precisely in dreams, where a person is disconnected from his daily routines and activities. While other books, such as *Sha'arei K'dusha* (Gates of Holiness), describe a dichotomy between the ordinary, temperamental psyche and its spiritual aspirations, *Sefer Hahizyonot* reveals a human view, including anger, conflicts and quarrels, and not only tranquility and hidden holiness.

RABBI JOSEPH CARO AND MAGGID MEISHARIM

Many know of Rabbi Joseph Caro thanks to his widely accepted halachic masterpiece – the *Shulchan Aruch*. Rabbi Caro published it within the context of a larger work, the *Beit Yosef*, based on the book *Arba'a Turim* of Rabbi Yakov, son of the Rosh. Because of the length of the *Beit Yosef*, Rabbi Caro also composed the *Shulchan Aruch*, with the goal that it would be possible to reread it every 30 days. Despite the opposition that the book stirred up in its time, both because it omitted Ashkenazi customs and for fear that it would lead to shallowness and lack of in-depth study, the book was eventually accepted for all generations. Not many know that there are several famous rabbis who opposed reading the book and even instructed their students thus, including the Mahari Ben Lev and the Maharal of Prague, who opposed this book together with his brother and renowned scholar Rabbi Chaim.

But aside from his halachic works, Rabbi Joseph Caro wrote another book that included ethics, kabbalah, and Biblical commentary, entitled *Maggid Meisharim*. This is a sort of autobiographical journal in which he records revelations of a higher power that brings ideas and commentaries as well as halachot. The book is written mostly in Aramaic, together with some Hebrew words and a few Spanish words.

There is no scholarly consensus regarding the book's authorship, due to occasional contradictions between halachot appearing in this book and halachot appearing in the *Shulchan Aruch*. Despite many indications to prove that Caro was indeed its author, the historian Shlomo Rosanis holds that the authors were in fact Rabbi Eliyahu de Vidas, author of *Reishit Hochma*, and Rabbi Haim Vital, the Ari's student.

THE BOOK HAYAT KANEH

Rabbi Solomon Molcho lived from 1500 until 1532. He was a Crypto-Jew who was baptized as a Christian with the name of Diogo Pires in Portugal, and even served as secretary of the High Court of Appeals of King Manuel I. After meeting "the Jewish traveler" David Reubeni, who was presenting the Christians with a plan to establish a Jewish country, Pires returned to Judaism, hebraicized his name, and even circumcised himself. Rabbi Molcho was endowed with diligence and even "help from Above"; the breadth of knowledge in Judaism and kabbalah that he acquired in such a short time was seen as something miraculous by the kabbalists of his generation.

Rabbi Molcho wrote extensively on calculating the end of the world and attempts to bring about the Jews' salvation; together with David Reubeni he even tried to start an army of Marranos ("crypto Jews forced to convert to Christianity") from the Jewish communities in order to liberate the Land of Israel from the Ottoman Empire. Rabbi Molcho was executed at age 32 by the Inquisition, but before that he managed to write two books. One, *Sefer Hamefo'ar* (The Glorious Book), dealing with the coming of the Messiah and the redemption of Israel, was published a year before his death. The other, *Hayat Kaneh*, in which Rabbi Molcho describes the visions that appeared to him in dreams, was only published 130 years after his death.

In *Hayat Kaneh*, Rabbi Molcho describes how he learned the large amount of material that he knew in Torah and kabbalah; he said that things were shown to him "in visions in dreams, for there I was shown all the things that were to happen to me in the future."

Thus, for the kabbalists, dreams did not remain merely theoretical. Various rabbis and kabbalists used dreams to receive answers, prophesy the future, and communicate with higher powers that could not always be encountered in the waking state. But as in other cultures, mysticism leaves dreams to a few individuals, outstanding figures with the authority to interpret dreams and use them. This is the way of the occult – to be hidden away for a few privileged individuals. Judaism, however, also offers a way for the wider population to access dreams, charting the way for the multitudes, and based on the Talmud and halachic rulings.

This is what we will cover in the next chapter.

7

DREAMS IN THE BABYLONIAN TALMUD

DREAMS IN THE TALMUD

The Babylonian Talmud is a work that was begun in the third century CE and completed towards the end of the fifth century. This work is divided into 37 tractates and includes 2,711 pages bringing together two centuries of debates, misgivings, stories, laws, anecdotes, advice, studies, and a range of other aspects that offer a unique, dramatic glimpse of what was happening in the Jewish community, which succeeded in preserving itself and its customs for more than 2,000 years. To this day, Jews study the Babylonian Talmud, beginning from junior high school through organized learning in yeshivas and ending with daily learning that is integrated into an adult Jew's life. Dreams occupy a significant place in the Babylonian Talmud, and therefore, to explore this issue broadly, this chapter is dedicated to the various dreams and dreamers that appear in the Talmud.

We begin by migrating to Babylon

RABBA'S DREAMS THAT GIVE
SIGNIFICANCE TO DREAMS
The Dream of Abbayi and Rabba

The Babylonian Talmud, in Tractate Berachot (p. 56) speaks of finding "dream interpreters." Abbayi and Rabba[19] even go to a dream interpreter by the name of Bar Hadaya who would interpret dreams differently for each person who came to him. The interpretation of the dream – as positive or negative – depended on the payment. For someone who paid, the interpretation of his dream was positive, while someone who did not pay would get a negative interpretation. The Talmud recounts how Abbayi got good interpretations while Rabba, who avoided paying, got bad ones. This was repeated even when they had identical dreams containing the verse "Thine ox shall be slain before thine eyes, and thou shalt not eat thereof." (Deuteronomy 28:31) While for Abbayi, Bar Hadaya's interpretation was that he would merit fathering sons and daughters, marrying them off, and seeing "as though" they were captured and carried off; for Rabba, he said that his sons and daughters would actually be taken from him.

This occurred again with other verses and with other images and symbols that appeared in their dreams. After one of Bar Hadaya's interpretations came true for Rabba, and he was attacked by two blind men who were quarreling, Rabba decided to pay Bar Hadaya for interpreting the dreams. After paying, Rabba received good interpretations. Thus matters continued until Bar Hadaya's book for dream interpretation fell and it was found to contain the words "All dreams follow the mouth" (that is, dreams are influenced by the interpretation they are given). Enraged, Rabba cursed Bar

---

19   Abbayi and Raba were a pair of rabbis who lived between 280 and 350 CE. They had many disagreements that were brought up in the Talmud and their common mention is repeated many times there.

Hadaya, who decided to exile himself to Rome for fear of the sage's curse, and out of hope that his exile would atone for his iniquity.

It should be noted that, according to the Biblical commentator and philosopher Ibn Ezra (1089-1164), the theory that "all dreams follow the mouth" is one individual's viewpoint that has not been accepted as a traditional position on this issue.

In another story, Bar Hadaya decides to position himself at the entrance to the King's palace, where he interacts with the guard of the King's treasury. The Talmud recounts how the guard has dreams and Bar Hadaya refuses to interpret either the first one or the second one for free. Then the guard has a third dream, in which a worm eats his entire hand, and Bar Hadaya interprets this to mean that moths will eat all the King's garments. This in fact occurs, and the King's courtiers are enraged at the guard of the Treasury, who in turn accuses Bar Hadaya of refusing to give an interpretation earlier which, for the price of a *zuz* (a small coin), could have prevented the King's valuable garments from being spoiled. Bar Hadaya is sentenced to death.

Rabba and His Father's Dream

The Talmud in Tractate Ta'anit 24 describes how King Shapur sought to punish Rabba after a man died in Rabba's court from lashes that were decreed because the accused had had sexual relations with a non-Jewish woman. However, King Shapur's mother, Ifra Hormizd, prevented the king from punishing Rabba. She asked Rabba to prove his claim of a unique connection between God and the Jewish people, and demanded that he ask for rain to fall during the summer month of Tammuz, solely by the power of his prayer. After failing at first, Rabba kept imploring his Creator and eventually succeeded in bringing rain that both filled the gutters of Tzippori and continued all the way to the Tigris River. That same night, Rabba went to bed and, in his dream, his father reprimanded him for bothering God and getting Him to change the ways of nature. He advised Rabba to move to a different sleeping place so that destructive forces would not harm him. Awakening after the dream, Rabba followed his father's advice and discovered the next morning that there were signs of knife cuts on the bed he had vacated; thus he understood that his father's advice in the dream had been correct.

Rabba and Rabbi Safra's Dream

In Tractate Hulin (133a), the Talmud describes how Rabba (who was a priest) asked his servant to acquire for him the priestly gifts before they were legitimately given to him. At night, Rabbi Safra dreamt about the verse from Proverbs (25:20), "As one that taketh off a garment in cold weather, and as vinegar upon nitre, So is he that singeth songs to a heavy heart," which hints at a negative description of Rabba's behavior. Rashi explains that following Rabba's behavior in bringing rain, he was "rebuked in Heaven," and therefore he could not be shown this directly in his own dream.

The dream of Rabba and Rabbi Elazar of Hagronya

This dream is also mentioned in Tractate Ta'anit, where after a drought year, Rabba decreed a fast in a place called Hagronya, a town on the Euphrates. Despite the fast, the rain was delayed, and accordingly the community decided to continue the fast into their sleep, rather than ending it at nightfall as was customary. The next morning, Rabba gathered everyone together and asked if anyone had had a dream that night. Rabbi Eleazar Hagronya recounted that he had a dream in which these words appeared: "A good peace for a good rabbi from the Lord of Good who in His goodness has done good for His people." Hearing the dream, Rabba saw it as sign that this was a time of favor, and decided to continue the prayers until the rain began to fall.

Rabbi Meir Denies the Significance of Dreams

The Talmud describes Rabbi Meir[20] as someone who did not ascribe significance to dreams. In Tractate Gittin (52), there is a description of Rabbi Meir's neighbor, who was the legal guardian of orphans and who sold land in order to buy slaves. Rabbi Meir prevented him from doing so because slaves are defined as something temporary (not durable) in contrast to land (which is durable). Rabbi Meir had a dream in which there was opposition to his actions, in the form of a wondering question: "I am to destroy and you are to build?" However, Rabbi Meir did not accord significance to the dream and declared that the words of dreams do not have significance ("neither raise nor lower").

Tractate Horayot (13) tells of disagreements between Rabbi Meir and Rabbi Natan on the one side, and Rabban Shimon ben Gamliel, on the other. In this dispute, the former sought to prove their own honored position by raising challenging questions against the latter in Tractate Uktzim. This attempt led to their being expelled from the House of Study. Only after it was discovered that they were bringing in notes from the outside with questions and explanations that those sitting in the House of Study could not manage to solve, was it agreed to bring them in, with the caveat that in the future they would not be mentioned by name but rather called "others" (Rabbi Meir) and "some say" (Rabbi Natan). The Talmud recounts that Rabbi Natan and Rabbi Meir were shown in a dream

---

20 Rabbi Meir lived in the third century CE and is another rabbi who is mentioned many times in the Gemara. He was a descendant of Nero the Roman emperor (37-68 CE) who converted and became a Jew.

that they should go and make peace, but while Rabbi Natan obeyed the dream and went to make peace, Rabbi Meir refused, on the grounds that the words of dreams neither raise nor lower.

Rabbi Yossi ben Halafta Interprets Dreams

In Tractate Berachot, the Babylonian Talmud recounts that towards the end of the Second Temple Period, there were dream interpreters, like Bar Hadaya, who interpreted dreams for Abbayi and Rabba, as described above. But the Jerusalem Talmud (Ma'aser Sheni 4,6) notes that one of the dream interpreters was none other than Rabbi Yossi ben Halafta, who served as a fourth-generation Tanna (a teacher or scholar) in the second century and was one of Rabbi Akiva's students. Rabbi Yossi ben Halafta was ordained by Rabbi Yehuda ben Baba (Sanhedrin 14), in violation of a Roman edict, and after his ordination fled to Asia (Baba Metzia 74) until the decree was rescinded. Afterwards, he went to settle in Usha, which was the seat of the Sanhedrin court at that time.

Rabbi Yossi ben Halafta is better known as Rabbi Yossi of the Mishna, and the Talmud tells us that in a dispute between Rabbi Yossi and his companions, the Halacha is according to his opinion (Eruvin 46) – that he is right, because he provides justification for every ruling. Elsewhere it is noted that deciding a law according to Rabbi Yossi had a unique value (Pesachim 50). His arrival at Tzippori (a city in Northern Israel), where he founded a yeshiva that had many students, originally stemmed from a denunciation by Yehuda ben Gerim, who reported to the Romans on a conversation between Rabbi Yossi, Rabbi Shimon, and Rabbi Yehuda. In that conversation, Rabbi Yehuda praised the Romans for their public works, Rabbi Shimon observed that they did all those projects for their own sake, and Rabbi Yossi was silent. In response, the Romans decreed that Rabbi Yossi should be exiled because of his silence (in contrast to Rabbi Yehuda, to whom it was decided to give a higher position, while Rabbi Shimon, who had condemned the Romans, was sentenced to execution) (Shabbat 33).

OTHER DREAMS MENTIONED IN THE TALMUD

1. Rabban Yohanan ben Zakkai's dreams about his companions (Hagiga 14), as well as his dream on the night after Yom Kippur that his nephew would be forced to bring tribute to Caesar.

2. Rabbi Elazar's dream in Tractate B'horot (5). He dreamed about the figure of Rabbi Yohanan after they challenged his approach in the House of Study.

3. Rabbi Assi's dream (Baba Batra 143a) about Rabbi Huna bar Ivya, after Rabbi Ivya challenged his halachic ruling.

4. Rabbi Pappa's dream about the three students who did not accept his opinion, and he criticized their behavior, instructing them to distance themselves from him in order to save them from punishment.

5. Rabbi Abayu's dream (Jerusalem Talmud, Ta'anit 1,4).

6. Rabbi Nachman bar Yitzhak's dream (Yoma 22).

7. The dream of Rabbi Yehoshua, son of Rabbi Tanhum (Jerusalem Talmud, Shabbat 2,6).

Thus we have seen various dreams that appear in the Talmud and, in my opinion, the Talmud's innovation is that it shows the rich variety of dreams among the various rabbis. Not all dreams necessarily contain religious content; some reflect what is happening in the rabbis' daily lives. The direct encounter with these dreams, graphically described, allows us to look at these rabbinical figures through human eyes and reflect on the similarity between their dreams and ours, despite the different of almost two millennia between us.

So much for the essence of dreams. But what do we do when there are bad dreams? It turns out that Jewish law defines an entire religious ceremony around this issue.

8

DREAMS IN JEWISH LAW

RENDERING A DREAM BENIGN

Jewish law (*Halacha*) recognizes the unique influence of dreams on a person's mood, irrespective of the dream's content and what it hints at. Accordingly, there is a halachic ritual prescribed, known as "rendering a dream benign" (*hatavat ha- lom*), intended for someone who remembers a troubling dream. The ritual takes place at the conclusion of *shacharit* (the morning prayer) after the congregation leaves the synagogue. There is already something symbolic in this timing, which indicates the gap between the dream and the external reality. As with monetary laws, as well as the nullification of vows on the eve of Rosh Hashana and Yom Kippur, *hatavat halom* is performed before three men. In this case, there is no criterion for these men's qualifications other than that they are "people who love him." There is no consensus as to whether the dreamer must tell them the dream or whether they must interpret it, or whether he is only required to recall the dream in his thoughts. The dreamer says to them, "*Halma tavah hazai*" (I dreamed a good dream) – despite the fact that the dream was apparently not good for him. It appears that declaring the dream as good is intended to activate the principle that "All dreams go according to the mouth." The Talmud, in Tractate Berachot 55, continues that the "dream delegation" answers him "*Sh'tava hu v'tava lihvei rachmana lishveh letav, sheva zimnin ligzaru alach min shmaya, delihvei tava veihveh tava*" (It is good and it will be good, may God make it good, seven times may it be decreed for you from Heaven that it will be good and it will be good). Regarding the words "seven times may it be decreed for you from Heaven," there is a dispute as to how many times it must be said – seven times or three; the dispute surrounds the essence of the statement in the ritual and whether or not it is part of a "whisper" ritual that is said seven times.

After that, there is a long series of verses that the same "dream delegation" recites, concluding with the verse "Go thy way, eat thy bread with joy." (Eccl. 9:7) This concluding verse refers to the end of the dream's influence and freeing up of the dreamer's thoughts for other things. Evidence of how much the Sages considered dreams to affect people, despite differing approaches, is the fact that it is permissible to perform this ritual on the Sabbath, even though it is something private that normally would be forbidden on the Sabbath (it is forbidden to pray for personal needs on the Sabbath); this permission is explained on the basis of the principle of "saving a life" (*Knesset Hag'dolah*, 288; *Elia Rabba*, 220).

The Jerusalem Talmud, in Tractate Berachot, states that Rabbi Yonah (in the name of Rabbi Tanhum ben Rabbi Hiya) would say the following prayer which was to be said by someone who had a "difficult dream" at night.

> *Master of the Universe, I am Yours and my dreams are Yours, I dreamed a dream and I do not know what it is. May it be Your*

will, my God and God of my fathers, that all my dreams about me and about all of Israel shall be for good, whether I dreamed about myself or dreamed about others, and whether others dreamed about me; if they are good, strengthen and empower them, and may they come true for me and for them like the dreams of Joseph the Righteous; and if they need healing, heal them like Hizkiyahu King of Yehuda from his illness, and like Miriam the Prophetess from her leprosy, and like Na'aman from his leprosy, and like the Waters of Bitterness by Moses our Teacher, and the waters of Jericho by Elisha. And like You turned the wicked Bilaam's curse into a blessing, so turn all my dreams about me and about all of Israel to the good, and protect me and have mercy on me and be pleased with me. Amen.

There are several interesting anecdotes regarding this prayer.

First of all, the Jerusalem Talmud does not specify *when* this prayer is to be recited. The Babylonian Talmud, however, states that the prayer is recited during the Priestly Blessing, such that the petitioner completes the prayer at the same time that the priests finish their blessing, and thus the congregation that responds "Amen" to the Priestly Blessing responds "Amen" to his prayer as well. The Talmud suggests that the prayer be recited by anyone who had a dream and did not know what he saw. That means that in contrast to the *hatavat halom*, which is performed for a dream that the person remembers, before three people who love him, this prayer is for a case in which a person has only the impression of a significant dream, without any memory of what happened in the dream.

Second, the prayer's *location* in the service. In *nusach Eretz Yisrael*[21] prayer books that were found in the Cairo Geniza, the prayer

---

21   The text of the prayer based on the Cairo Geniza.

appears at the end of the morning blessings or after *Psukei D'zimra* (Verses of Song). Some researchers believe that the appearance of the prayer in this part of the prayer book shows that the prayer was common in the Land of Israel, and not exceptional like in the prayer books from Babylon, in which it appears very rarely, if at all.

Third, the fact of its importance. Maimonides did not rule that this prayer is Halacha and avoided mentioning it in his *Mishneh Torah*. Nevertheless, due to the mention of it by other *Rishonim* such as the Rif [22] and the Rosh,[23] it took root in various Jewish communities. Rabbi Yisrael of Radin, author of *Chafetz Haim* and *Mishna Berura*, states that in his community, the whole congregation would recite this prayer together. This was due to a custom in some places outside of Israel not to recite the Priestly Blessing except on holidays, along with the assumption that every member of the community surely has a bad dream from time to time.

Fourth. Here, too, permission is given to deviate from generally accepted customs. While the priests raise their hands in blessing, it is generally forbidden to recite verses or personal prayers. Despite this blanket prohibition, the prayer on dreams was permitted on account of danger and due to the recognition of a dream's exceptional influence on a person's psyche. Someone who did not manage to say the prayer during the Priestly Blessing says an abbreviated version: "Mighty in place, residing in strength, You are peace and Your name is peace, may it be Your will to place peace upon us."

This prayer accords a new religious significance to dreams. While the Talmud indicates that dreams do not necessarily come from "another world" and often rather reflect a person's personal

---

22 Rif is the nickname of Rabbi Yitzchak ben Ya'akov Alfasi (1103-1013) who lived in Algiers and then in Spain and is considered one of the greatest arbiters of Jewish law.

23 Rosh is the initials of Rabbi Asher ben Yehiel (1250-1327), who lived in Ashkenaz (now Cologne in Germany) and then in Toledo and is considered a judge and commentator who had a decisive influence on the shaping of Jewish law.

misgivings, this prayer ritual is a response to the experience and impression that a dream leaves on the dreamer. Jewish law understands that not everything passes through the intellect, and sometimes experience and emotion are stronger than anything else. Accordingly, a ritual with religious elements is allowed in an attempt to restore the spirit of someone who awakens from the effect of a troubling dream.

A dream is not only an event in itself; sometimes it requires a religious ritual to recover from it. A dream can also trigger halachic misgivings, or be a means of resolving a doubt that the person has not managed to resolve while awake. A dream, in fact, can sometimes be further refined by focusing on its rational aspect, while adding a mystical-practical side that represents another aspect of the world of dreams.

USING DREAM QUERIES TO CLARIFY HALACHIC QUESTIONS

Dreams appear in the Bible in a number of versions, with apparently contradictory statements regarding their significance. The Talmud in Tractate Berachot (55) deals with the contradiction between the verse in Zechariah "And the dreams speak falsely" (Zechariah 10:2) and what is said in the Book of Numbers, "I do speak with him in a dream." (Numbers 12:6)

The use of dream queries to clarify halachic questions – and not just directions and prophetic signs or signs foretelling the future – took shape during the Geonim Period. Legitimizing dreams as a halachic tool can be mainly ascribed to the work of Rabbeinu Yakov of Marvège, one of the Ba'alei Tosafot, who composed an entire work of responsa based on dreams, called *Responsa from Heaven.* Throughout this opus, Rabbi Yakov uses dozens of cases in order to rule on the most widespread questions in the halachic tradition. Thus, for example, Rabbi Yakov seeks to resolve the dispute between the approaches of Rashi and Rabbeinu Tam regarding the order of the Biblical texts in tefillin. In his response to this question, he states that there is no conclusive resolution to this dispute, that even God and his entourage are divided on this question. Some rabbis and halachic adjudicators cite the halachot written in this work, while others make a point of avoiding it because the responsa are based solely on dreams, without any broad halachic justification.

Rabbi Moshe of Coucy, one of the Ba'alei Tosafot from the thirteenth century, in the introduction to his book *Sefer Mitzvot Gadol* (Great Book of Commandments), known as the *Samag*, states that despite pleas over many years, he had avoided writing a book. However, he writes, "At the beginning of the sixth millennium, a vision came to me in a dream: Get up and do a *Sefer Torah* (a Torah scroll) in two parts!" We see here how one of the most significant halachic works also began with a dream. In addition, the *Samag* also makes use of a dream in the section dedicated to things forbidden by the Torah that are prefaced by the word "*lo*" (do not) and are therefore called the "*lavim*" (the do nots). In the chapter on such forbidden acts (64), he attributes a subsection of the chapter to something that was revealed to him in a dream. Similar things appear in *Shem Hagedolim* (Name of the Great Ones) of the Hida (in the entry on Maimonides), who describes how on the night after Maimonides finished writing the *Mishneh Torah* – which took him 10 years – his father appeared to him in a dream, together with another man whom his father introduced as Moses our Teacher, who had come to see the book that Maimonides had written.

Rabbi David Segal, author of *Turei Zahav* (*Taz*), states in *Even Ha'ezer* (121, Section 70) that the *Or Hazarua* (the nickname for the halachic work by Rabbi Yitzhak ben Moshe of Vienna) expressed uncertainty as to how the name Akiva should be spelled – whether it should end with the letter *heh* or *aleph*. The solution came to him in a dream when he saw the verse "Light is sown for the righteous and joy for the upright of heart," which in Hebrew ends in the letter *heh*, and from this he derived a ruling that the name Akiva should be written with a *heh*, even in a get (a divorce decree).

Rabbi Segal (commonly known as the Taz) also mentions a personal dream in another place. In *Orach Haim*, Section 585, after citing the Tur on the significance of the shofar blasts on Rosh Hashana and their effect on the entire year, the Taz writes:

> *Once in a dream an interpretation came to me of the verse "With trumpets and sound of the horn [shofar] Shout ye before the King, the LORD" via the Talmud's interpretation that people should be careful to blow the truah [sound] on the shofar before there is a shofar-blowing, God forbid, by the Holy One, Blessed be He, at the end of the year, and this is the meaning of "before the King, the LORD," that is to say, before the shofar-blowing of the Holy One, Blessed be He, God forbid.*

Even though he could have refrained from mentioning the dream, given its interpretative significance, the Taz still decided to mention the things that came to him in a dream. Thus we see the importance that halachic *poskim* (adjudicators) ascribed to their dreams, despite the apparent contradiction between halachic rationality and the mystery shrouding dreams.

There is an interesting trend in which, despite the Sages' statement that "dreams do not raise or lower" as well as the lack of meaning ascribed to things appearing in dreams, rabbis and halachic *poskim* still relied on things that appeared in dreams in order to resolve specific uncertainties. Below we will look at a few of the famous cases in which dreams were connected to halachic rulings.

PROHIBITION ON EATING LOCUSTS

Rabbi Chaim ben Atar, author of the commentary *Ohr HaChaim Al HaTorah*, wrote a halachic paper called *Pri To'ar*. In Section 85 he tells us there was a plague of locusts in his time tha caused great damage to the crops, and adds that, at that time, many permitted themselves to eat the locusts. Rabbi ben Atar reprimanded them and succeeded in leading many residents of his city away from this practice, except for one person. The person who had permitted himself to eat them had a dream that he was eating insects and detestable things, and understood that this represented the locusts that he had eaten that day.

A DREAM THAT BROUGHT A WARNING TO PREVENT A DISASTER

In the *Tashbatz Responsa*, in the context of discussing his banishment in a dream, Rabbi Shimon ben Tzemach tells the following story:

> *And know that it is almost twenty years ago that Hakon ben Abu, who today has left the Jewish faith, dreamed a dream that the community had to fast three fasts, Monday and Thursday and Monday and Rabbi Yitzhak bar Sheshet, may he be remembered for eternal life, was afraid of it and decreed 3 fasts and you see that the man's end proved his beginning because even at the beginning he was not a good person and the Rabbi, z"l (of blessed memory) should not have decreed those fasts and the community was insulting and ridiculing them and calling them dream fasts*

*and at the Mincha prayer we scarcely had a minyan and the
Rabbi z"l regretted that and I was fasting and saying that I know
myself that I am not a priest but if my friends tell me to go up
and lead the prayer I would go (Shabbat 118b) and the Rabbi z"l
explained why he required this, telling us that earlier, in Kalinsia,
the city where he was born, Shlomo from Tish came to him and
told him to decree a fast because he saw a big fire in the house of
the Rabbi z"l. And he was not afraid of his words at all and then
regretted it when he saw that the dream came true.*
(Responsa Tashbatz, Part 2, Section 128)

That is, Rabbi Yitzhak bar Sheshet (known as the Ribash) decrees a fast on the basis of one man in the community named Hakon ben Abu, who had left the Jewish faith. He is told in his dream that the community must fast three fasts on Monday, Thursday, and the following Monday. The community wonders why they have to fast on the basis of one commoner's dream and they do not want to observe the fast according to his dream. The Ribash explains that before this decree, in his birthplace of Calinesia, Shlomo of Tish came to him and told him to decree a fast because in his dream he saw a fire in the Rabbi's house. The Rabbi was unconcerned by his words but subsequently the dream came to pass, and therefore he regretted not having listened.

In another place, in Part 2, Section 159, the author of the *Tashbatz Responsa* mentions another dream he had:

*One night I had a dream in which I was eating impure things
and I was standing and trembling and my soul was grieved,
and lo the servant who buys me meat brought me meat that day
and told me jokingly Here is the forbidden and permitted meat,*

I said to him how, he said to me There is a sign of a blow on the wall, then I said this is the impure thing I ate in my dream, I commanded him to return it and since then I have been wary of similar things and have forbidden them for myself.

A DREAM WARNING REGARDING A HALACHIC RULING CONCERNING A BARBUTA FISH

One of the great students of the Maharam of Rothenburg was Rabbi Shimshon ben Tzadok, who accompanied the Maharam of Rothenburg during his stay in jail and documented his behavior, his customs, and his Torah insights in his book *Tashbatz Katan*. Rabbi Shimshon recounts a story connected to a dream:

I found in the name of Rabbeinu Baruch who told that once Rabbeinu Ephraim z"l ate some fish called barbuta and at night an old man appeared to him with long grey hair and a beatific expression and a long beard and brought him a container full of insects. And told him Get up and eat and he recoiled and he said Aren't those insects and he told him thus, they are permitted like the insects you ate today. When he woke up he knew that Eliyahu may he be remembered for good had appeared to him and from that day forward he stayed away from them. [From this some interpret that there are two kinds and those in France have scales under the ears. And there are also countries in which the whole fish is covered with scales but they fall off when it is taken out of the water and can be seen in the cloth when it is put in the net. But my teacher Rabbeinu Yehiel would not eat fish cooked with it.]
(Sefer Tashbatz Katan, Section 352)

In contrast, Rabbi Yehezkel Landau, author of the *Noda Biyehuda*, chose to relate to this dream differently. He refrained from ascribing unique meaning to the fact that the dream appeared specifically to Rabbeinu Ephraim, relating it instead to an interpretation that was given him:

> "I say: Things in dreams do not have significance, and I never heard of halachic decisions made from this master of dreams, and "the dreams speak falsely." And if Rabbeinu Ephraim z"l was a righteous man and a great Hassid, and was concerned about his dream – that he was told in his dream that he had permitted the insect and he was afraid lest that was true and connected it to the fact that he permitted the barbuta fish – at any rate if Rabbi Ephraim had verified that this fish had scales, as the Ba'alei Tosafo verified it, he would have connected the interpretation of his dream to some other matter that he had permitted and was concerned about. But to bring proof from a passing dream – that is futile, it is not real. And I respectfully ask the great rabbi, why did this master of dreams not come to the other Ba'alei Tosafot and to Rabbeinu Tam and the great poskim who permitted barbuta and reveal his dream to them so they could see what was in his dreams." For everything follows the interpretation, the dream is rolled around and its interpretation changed until the interpretation fits some reality. Thus says the Noda Biyehuda that if Rabbeinu Ephraim had clarified that barbuta has scales, he would have simply gone and interpreted his dream differently. (Responsa Noda Biyehuda (Tanina Edition – Yoreh Deah, Section 30)).

UNITING AND UNITY OF THE FOUR SPECIES

Rabbi Joseph Caro largely kept his kabbalistic side separate from his halachic side. Throughout his books *Shulchan Aruch* and *Beit Yosef,* mysticism scarcely appears and his halachic rulings rely on specific laws. Despite this dichotomy, Rabbi Caro sometimes introduces mysticism and kabbalah in his halachic rulings, often choosing to correspond with various kabbalistic-halachic rulings. One interesting ruling appears in the *Beit Yosef's* deliberations on whether to hold the *etrog* (citron) together with the other species during the waving, or whether the etrog should be held by only the left hand while the *lulav* (palm branch together with myrtle and willow) is waved with the right hand. He resolves this doubt via a dream:

> *Does the etrog need to be connected to the lulav during the waving, waving the two together, or should only the bundle of the lulav be waved alone while the left hand, holding the etrog, remains still without waving? This question is not clarified in the Talmud nor in the words of the poskim but Rabbi Menachem Ricanati wrote in Parshat Emor ... And this secret was revealed to me in a dream on the night of the first holiday of Sukkot when an Ashkenazi Hassid was staying with me named Rav Rebbe Itzhak, in a dream I saw that he was writing the name Yud Heh and was distancing the last heh from the first three letters and I asked him What did you do? And he answered: Thus they do in our place. And I protested and wrote it whole and I was amazed at the sight and could not understand. The next day, when taking the lulav, I saw that he was shaking only the lulav and its bundled species without the etrog and I understood the interpretation of my dream and changed my mind and our Sages hinted at this secret in Vayikra Rabba...* (Beit Yosef Orech Haim, Section 651)

That is, the Beit Yosef starts from the assumption that the four species represent the four letters making up God's name (*yod, heh, vav, heh*). In any case, he considered that separating the *etrog* from the other three species, which is more convenient for the person waving the *lulav*, is like erasing God's four-letter name. This has an additional meaning, given the comparison of the four species to four ranks and/or levels in the population, with the *etrog* likened to a righteous person since it is the only one of the four species that has both taste and smell. Separating the *etrog* (= the righteous person) from the rest of the species (= the rest of the Jewish people) is like erasing God's name and losing the unity of its four letters on account of this separation.

THE RADBAZ'S RESPONSA CONCERNING THE DISPUTE OVER TEFILLIN BETWEEN RABBEINU TAM AND RASHI

> *I was asked whether a person who has tefillin according to Rabbeinu Tam's opinion and wants to make them accord with the opinion of Rashi z"l, whether there is a concern that this might be forbidden:*
>
> *Response: Even though this has no aspect of nullification, since even according to Rabbeinu Tam they must be written in order and the dispute is only regarding what order they are placed in the boxes, still there is something forbidden because it is disrespectful to those who hold this opinion, for according to them the tefillin are kosher and to declare them unkosher reduces their holiness and there is no greater prohibition than this ... And I was asked about this and I instructed that it is permitted and that night*

*I was shown in a dream that I had not instructed correctly and
I changed my mind on this matter and saw that it contained
disrespect for all the great rabbis and therefore I decree that it is
forbidden to do so halachically, for the reasons I have written.*
(Responsa of Radbaz, Part 6, Section 2 2286)

PERMITTING AGUNOT VIA A DREAM

One of the most complex issues in Halacha is declaring an *aguna*[24]
free to marry again. In Judaism, from the moment a woman decides
to marry a man, she cannot be released from the marriage unless
she obtains a *get* (divorce decree) from him or he dies. An *aguna*
is a woman who cannot marry another man, either because her
husband has disappeared or because he is legally unfit to give her
a *get*. If the woman has sexual relations with another man while
still an *aguna* she is considered to be an adulteress, which is seen
as an extremely serious violation of Halacha. It exposes her to
severe halachic sanctions, including the inability to marry the man
with whom she had relations, as well as defining her offspring as
unmarriageable – *mamzerim*.[25]

Rabbinic literature is full of challenging descriptions of rabbis
who struggled intensively until they succeeded in finding a solution
for disentangling an *aguna* from her situation. One such instance
appears in the book of responsa *Meshivat Nefesh* of the eighteenth-
century Rabbi Aryeh Leib Tzintz. In this case, three married men
drowned in a boat, leaving no trace. Rabbi Aryeh Leib's response
is that in the case of drowning, the size of the lake/river/sea is very

---

24 "Aguna" is a term for a married woman whose husband's whereabouts are unknown and she cannot
    marry or live with another man because of this uncertainty.

25 A bastard is a halakhic-religious-Jewish status for someone born from sexual intercourse of a
    married woman with another man. The bastard status prevents him from marrying other Jews but
    only a bastard like himself. The reason for this attitude is the great importance Judaism places on
    preserving the marriage bond and rejecting infidelity.

significant, and whether it is "a body of water that has an end" or
"a body of water that has no end." In addition, it is significant that
many halachic questions that were asked that related to events in
a period when modern communication technology did not yet
exist, thus posing difficulties in communication, even if the men in
question were in fact saved. And indeed, one of the cases that came
before Rabbi Tzedaka Hotzin – a student of the Ben Ish Chai who
served as a judge in the Eida Haredit religious court – involved a
dream regarding a levirate association (marriage of a man to his late
brother's childless widow). In the case brought to Rabbi Hotzin, a
man from Baghdad whose children had died said on his deathbed
that he had a brother in a distant place in the cities of Ashkenaz
and he did not know whether the brother was dead or alive. When
he was asked a second time later on, he said that he had dreamed
that his brother was dead, and Rabbi Hotzin was asked whether the
dream could be relied on and therefore whether the wife could be
released from her obligation to the levirate marriage.

> *Things in dreams do not have significance [lit. "do not raise and*
> *do not lower"]. If so, his first words are the main thing, when he*
> *said that he has a brother and does not know whether he is dead*
> *or alive. If so, we assume that he exists as long as it is not known*
> *that he has died, like the law concerning someone who brings a get*
> *from a country across the sea, that we assume that the man exists.*
> (Tzedaka u'Mishpat Responsa, Even Ha'ezer, Section 48)

In contrast, in Rabbi Tzintz's case, the mother of one of the men
on the boat dreamed of her drowned son, indicating signs in the
dream that enabled identification of his possessions. On the basis
of the dream, Rabbi Tzintz was asked to permit the three *agunot*

to remarry. Despite mentioning the Talmudic dictum that "things in dreams do not raise or lower," Rabbi Tzintz decided to make an exception and rely on the dream in order to permit the *aguna* to get married to another man:

> *Here is a dream that the woman dreamed, the mother of the*
> *drowned man... it does not appear to be an empty thing... In this*
> *marvelous dream, which gave appropriate advice how to find him*
> *using metal tools, and provided several marks and signs, so that*
> *it definitely appears to be a true vision... And in Perek Haroeh*
> *it is stated that dreams have reality for a number of matters. Also*
> *we should not say that this dream was just the cogitations of her*
> *heart, because the woman herself never thought of it ... not at all.*
> *And from the Talmud... which said that "Things in dreams do not*
> *count ..." this is regarding expropriation of money, for which even*
> *a single witness is not considered reliable... [but] for the matter*
> *of permitting a woman, in which we rely even on a witness who*
> *heard it from another witness who heard from a servant woman,*
> *it seems we should permit it based on a dream which appears to*
> *be true... for a dream is more reliable than one witness if it has*
> *signs and reglai'im l'dvar [relates to two cases that appear to be*
> *connected], only that it cannot be used to expropriate a person's*
> *money. And if so, if we believe testimony of a witness who heard*
> *it from another witness who heard from a servant woman,*
> *there is no doubt that one should rely on a dream which contains*
> *signs and symbols and marks of water that has no end, that it is*
> *not just an issue where avoidance is recommended, rather, one*
> *should thoroughly rely on the section that I wrote about dreams.*

(Responsa Meshivat Nafesh, Section 35)

RABBI OVADIA YOSEF'S POSITION ON MAKING HALACHIC RULINGS BASED ON DREAMS

Rabbi Ovadia Yosef (Sephardi Chief Rabbi of Israel from 1973 to 1983) was considered to have been one of the most outstanding figures of the twentieth century in making halachic rulings and laying out a halachic path. He opposed giving mystical meaning to dreams, and chose to relate to dreams only from their narrow halachic aspect – fasting in response to a bad dream. Rabbi Ovadia Yosef would say that even when a dream appears to have spiritual significance, kabbalists have said that dreams are intermingled with other things and can even come from demons. (*Yachaveh Da'at*, 4,24)

Rabbi Ovadia Yosef's own rabbi, Rabbi Yakov Haim Sofer, named Kaf HaChaim after the book he wrote, would incorporate dreams into Halacha (91,45; 232,6). He compiled these things in a book, *Kuntres*[26] *of Dreams*, which exists in a notebook in his hand-writing. This notebook, kept by Rabbi Ovadia Yosef, contains close to 800 dreams-visions that appeared to him in dreams.

Accordingly, he did not accept the halachic approach of the thirteenth-century Rabbi Yakov Sofer of Marvège's book of responsa, *Min Hashamayim* (Reponsa from Heaven), which constitutes halachic rulings and a halachic approach to dreams. This is in contrast to the Hida (rabbinical scholar Chaim Yosef David Azulai), who relied on the rulings of Rabbi Yakov of Marvège. Regarding *Min Hashamayim*, Rabbi Ovadia Yosef came out very strongly against this approach and the trend to rely on things that appear in dreams:

> *Someone who reads closely will see immediately that the halacha*
> *should not rely on the rulings brought in the responsa Min Hasha-*

---

26   Kuntres is a term for the composition of a pamphlet or booklet, as opposed to a book.

mayim... About this they said: It is not from heaven. And the
teaching was given only to the Sages of Israel who would decide
according to the rules of the teaching. In particular, all the rulings
that were brought in the responsa Min Hashamayim were made
by querying a dream, and they already said... Things in dreams
do not have significance. And in the book Shibbolei Haleket
(Section 157), a passage from the responsa Min Hashamayim was
brought, and it was written regarding it that one should not pay
attention to the things in dreams, because "it is not in heaven."
And also in the responsa of Noda b'Yehuda, Tanina (Yoreh Deah,
Section 30) that one should not take into account things in dreams,
even in the dream of a great man, and even to be more strict, let
alone to be more lenient.

It is interesting to note that in 2001 a furor arose in the Haredi community, publicized in various newspapers, following a statement by Rabbi Ovadia Yosef in which he recounted that he had dreamed that the Messiah was at the Western Wall. Following that dream, Rabbi Ovadia Yosef initiated a special convocation at the Porat Yosef Yeshiva in Jerusalem. The fact that Rabbi Ovadia Yosef is considered a rationalist and someone who fought against those who sanctified dreams and mysticism, gave this dream unique significance at that time

HALACHOT THAT RESULTED FROM DREAMS
Eating Bread
One of every person's daily activities is the eating of bread. In Judaism, bread is considered to be a food that halachically defines a meal, thus requiring ritual hand-washing before eating and the blessing *Birkat Hamazon* afterwards. Bread has great symbolism,

expressing a person's labor; holding the loaf with two hands while saying the blessing indicates the 10 *mitzvot* (commandments) that a person performs before the grain becomes bread. In many ways, bread also represents the realization of Adam's punishment: "In the sweat of thy face shalt thou eat bread, till thou return unto the ground; for out of it wast thou taken." (Genesis 3:19)

One of the most basic halachot regarding breaking a loaf of bread is connected to a dream – not just any dream, but a dream featuring Menashe, son of Heftzibah and Hezkiyah, king of Yehuda. In the Book of Kings and in the Book of Chronicles, Menashe is described as cancelling the prophets' sweeping religious reforms, sinning with idol worship, and introducing the worship of Ba'al and Ashera into Judaism. Various midrashim indicate additional sins that Menashe committed, such as the murder of his grandfather, the prophet Isaiah, erasing God's name from Torah scrolls, and having sexual relations with his sister. In no fewer than four places in the Bible his sins are mentioned as the cause of the First Temple's destruction. (Kings II, 21:12-14, 23; 26; Jeremiah 15:4)

After the fourth-century Rabbi Ashi expressed disdain for Ahab, Jeroboam, and Menashe, he had a dream in which Menashe admonished him, saying that he was greater than the rabbi in his knowledge of Halacha, and that Rabbi Ashi did not know where to break a loaf of bread. The Talmud, in Tractate Sanhedrin 102, recounts that after Rabbi Ashi did not respond, Menashe provided him with the answer, saying that the bread must be broken in the place *"d'karim bishula"* (there are several interpretations and versions of this response, and we will settle for the interpretation of Maimonides and the *Shulchan Aruch*, which understand Menashe to say that it is well baked). Rabbi Ashi responded that he would teach this ruling in his House of Study in Menashe's name. The contents of the dream became more than a mere tale: it was ruled as Halacha in the *Shulchan Aruch.* (Orech Chayim 167:1)

Requesting Forgiveness Before Being Called to the Torah

Rabbi Moshe Teitelbaum, one of the most outstanding rabbis of Hungary in the eighteenth and nineteenth centuries, is widely known for his masterpiece on the Bible, *Yismach Moshe.* In his book *Yayin Harekach* on the halachot of *Orech Chayim*, Rabbi Teitelbaum writes, in *Orech Chayim*, Section 141, "He dreamed that the one reading the Torah publicly must first forgive all of Israel, so that he should have no resentment in his heart against any Jew.

Bringing a Corpse from Outside Israel to Be Buried in Israel According to a Dream

An interesting question appears in the writing of Rabbi Moshe Stern, who survived the Holocaust and became one of the most famous halachic *poskim* in Brooklyn in the twentieth century. In his *Be'er Moshe*, he published many of the questions asked of him during his lifetime, including one connected to a dream. In this dream, the father appears to the son and demands to be removed from his burial place and brought to the Land of Israel for burial; the son asks if he is obligated in this matter. One can note Rabbi Stern's personal comment about how shocked he was by the very question:

> *I was asked by one of the householders of Borough Park and I was shocked by the question. For his father who died a few years earlier, while still alive, had mentioned to his son and his son-in-law in an idle conversation that if he died it would be good if they brought him to the Land of Israel for burial. And their father was then young (about 50) and they got angry with him – as it is the*

*way of a son and son-and-law to get discouraged about something
like that – saying why is he saying such things, but they remembered his words, and after a few years his life ended and he passed
away. And they could not bring him to Israel. And now his father
came in a dream and asked him to fulfill his wish from when he
was alive, even though he did not command him while he was
alive, but reminded him of his wish, and now he came to ask
whether he is obligated or not. And the main obstacle comes from
his mother, may she live, who does not want to bring on herself
a renewed period of mourning, particularly because she has heart
disease. Of course if he had asked her she would have agreed and
moreover would have asked to fulfill her husband's wish, that is,
his father's wish.... Therefore I said why should this be prolonged
more, although I still have a lot to say, follow the Sde Hemed [a
19th century Torah commentator] and find calm for your soul [...]
with the help of God, the One who gives human beings intelligence. And I found (there in Sde Hemed starting with the words
"Od matzati") who brought from the responsa Chaim b'Yad (from
the Gaon HaVif [Haim Palachi] Section 52) who was asked
regarding someone who made a vow in a dream to write a Torah
scroll in his name, whether he was obligated to fulfill his vow and
after expanding somewhat on the subject he concluded thus: the
person who vowed is obligated to write a Torah scroll as he vowed,
whether he himself dreamed that he made the vow or whether
someone else dreamed of him making the vow, and here his words
end.* (Responsa Be'er Moshe, Part 3, Section 171)

Issues of loans and inheritances

Poskim of Halacha relate to dreams in which deceased people
appear and clarify the nature of the inheritance that they left as

in the Talmud in Tractate Sanhedrin (30), which tells of someone who was troubled regarding the money left him by his father; his father came to him in a dream and said that this belongs to so and so and this is *ma'aser sheni* [a tithe] and the Talmud rules that this is meaningless since "Things in dreams have no significance." From here, the *Shulchan Aruch* (*Hoshen Mishpat* 255,9) also concludes that when the deceased left an inheritance and its location was unknown and he appeared in a dream, it does not have any meaning since dreams "do not have any significance."

Excommunication and Vows in Dreams

The Talmud in Tractate Nedarim (8) discusses someone who was excommunicated in a dream, and states that he must obtain a nullification of the excommunication via a quorum of 10 men. This statement was ruled as Halacha (Shulchan Aruch, Yorei Dea, 334, 35) and the Radbaz states in the name of the Geonim that for someone who dreamed on the Sabbath that he was ex- communicated, it is considered to be a great need and therefore he can be permitted to nullify the vow on the Sabbath. When someone decided to vow to refrain and take on a strict observance, such as not eating *matza shruya* (matza that has absorbed liquid) on Pesach, the Hatam Sofer (Yorei Dea, 222,3) instructed that he must take on the strict observance. The same holds for an active dream in which the person dreamed that he swore or vowed that he would ask a Torah scribe to write a Torah scroll for him; Rabbi Haim Pallaci ruled that he must fulfill his oath (*Responsa Haim b'Yad*, 52). The same applies to a dream in which someone vows to give charity; he must fulfill the vow (*Responsa Mishneh Halachot Tanina*, 2, 112; *Responsa Dovev Meisharim*, 3, 85) or buy a beautiful *etrog* (*Responsa Be'er Moshe* 3,170,3).

Performing a Mitzvah in a Dream

Despite the spiritual significance of dreams, halachic *poskim* clarified that someone who dreamed that he performed a mitzvah or said a blessing, such as counting the *omer*, did not fulfill the mitzvah and he must count the *omer* again with a blessing (Lev Haim 3,121; (*Tzedek Yesod Olam* 20,27). Also, when a person dreamed that he was thirsty and said the *shehakol*[27] blessing and immediately afterwards woke up and felt thirsty, he should say the blessing again; the blessing he said in his dream does not count (*Pri Hasadeh*, 2, 107).

The Hazon Ish explains that this also applies to someone who read all of the *Kriyat Sh'ma* in a dream and wants to rely on that reading. Since it did not take place while he was awake and should not be accorded any significance, he cannot rely on it and must read the entire prayer again (Orech Hayim, 9,8).

SUMMARY

Rabbinical Signs and Criteria for Distinguishing Between Various Dreams or When to Be Concerned About a Dream

Despite the statement that things in dreams do not raise or lower, the *Rishonim* displayed a wide range of positions on when one should be concerned about something in a dream and act accordingly.

The Ritva [Yom Tov ben Avraham of Seville](Tractate Ta'anit 12,2, in the sentence beginning "Rav Yehoshua") offers the criterion that when a person is "panicked and frightened" in a dream about some personal matter, it is "certainly a message from Heaven" to examine his deeds and repent.

Abarbanel [Isaac ben Yehuda, 15th century], in his commentary on the Torah (Bereishit, 41) states that there are two criteria for distinguishing between significant and non-significant dreams.

---

27   A type of blessing that Jews say before they eat some of the food.

These are both subjective signs, or, as he says, "independent signs." One relates to the dreamer himself, whether he is clear and correct and not confused by foreign things that he saw. The other is whether the dreamer experiences a feeling of significant amazement that is not mere false imagination. This amazement is also mentioned in the Torah, in regards to both Pharaoh and Nebuchadnezzar, "And his spirit was troubled." (Genesis 41:8 and Daniel 2:1)

Rabbeinu Bachya (Genesis 41:1) says that dreams come either due to foods eaten, or due to thoughts, or to strengthen the soul. When the dream comes to strengthen the soul, it is a "small prophecy" that can come to the wicked as well as to the righteous, and in the dream, the dreamer feels clarity, as though he "sees it in reality."

The Rashba (*Responsa of the Rashba*, 1,483) holds that the decision on whether or not to accord significance to a dream should be based on whether there are signs in the dream that come true (that is, some of the things in the dream come to pass in reality); in this case, one should be concerned about the remaining things in the dream.

She'iltot d'Rav Achai Geon (Part 1, Section 29) and *Responsa* of the Rashbatz [Simeon ben Tzemach Duran, 14th-15th centuries] (2, 128) distinguish between matters related to money, in which one should not accord significance to a dream, and matters related to prohibitions, in which one should be concerned about the things in the dream.

Sefer Hahasidim (Section 727) states that one should be concerned about all dreams, and the Sages' saying that "Dreams do not raise or lower" refers specifically to *mitzvot*.

Rabbi Jonathan of Lunel (Commentary on the Rif, 8.2) states that the distinction is who had the dream; for one's own dreams, one must always be concerned about the content and believe it while one does not need to believe other people's dreams.

The Maharsha (Berachot 18,2, with the sentence beginning with "*Ma'aseh*") says that one should be concerned about dreams that occur on the eve of Rosh Hashana, since this is the Day of Judgment, and therefore someone who has a bad dream must fast (the Maharsha mentions two places in the Talmud – Baba Batra 10 and Berachot 18 – in which people had dreams on Rosh Hashana and took the dreams seriously).

Rabbi Shmuel Landau, in the responsa *Shivat Tzion* (Section 52) states that the division is between the past and the future: one should not be concerned about dreams regarding the past, but should be concerned about dreams regarding the future.

Aruch Hashulchan (*Orech Haim*, Halachot Brachot Haperot, Section 220,1) and Rabbi Yekutiel Halberstam, in his responsa *Divrei Yatziv* (Yorei Deah 121) focus on the identity of the dreamer. Rabbi Halberstam says that the dream of a simple person is not like the dream of a righteous person, and thus he resolves the contradiction in the Sages' writings regarding dreams' significance and power.

Orchot Tzadikim, Sha'ar Ha'emet. There is no need to be concerned about dreams, but someone who trains himself to always have true thoughts will also see true visions in his dreams and will know the future as the angels know it.

Ohr Hahaim (Genesis 37:7) says that the criterion is clarity; when a dream is "clear as daylight," i.e., the dream's interpretation and its future realization are unequivocally clear, it is "a vision of God," i.e., a sort of prophecy granted to the dreamer.

EVERY JEWISH END IS A NEW BEGINNING

The survey of halachic rulings, in which rabbis ascribe practical elements to dreams, gives us a full perspective on how Judaism regards dreams. The Jewish conception includes both practical and mystical aspects, integrating philosophical and psychological worlds. Thus

Judaism sees dreams as an integral part of our lives, our decisions, and our choices. The law in the State of Israel is not Jewish, but rather represents a combination of Ottoman, German, British, and European law. Nevertheless, since the State of Israel is relatively young – 75 years old – its legal system is constantly undergoing innovations and is subject to ongoing disputes. We found there, of all places, a unique precedent regarding dreams, which we will discuss in the next chapter.

9

THE LAW OF DREAMS – DREAMS IN CRIMINAL LAW

It is quite surprising that dreams are missing from the world of law, which anchors social relationships and relates frequently to people's everyday events. This may be because dreams are considered to be irrational and, by their nature, difficult to verify. In the State of Israel, however, dreams have earned a special legal status in criminal law, due to the case of an Israeli woman who dreamed dreams in the U.S. and afforded us an interesting peek at the legal approach to dreams.

DREAMS AND LAW

Despite dreams' subjectivity and lack of reality, they have achieved a certain recognition and expression in the field of criminal law. This recognition has come about in cases of incest or the sexual abuse of women that was perpetrated in their childhoods. It should be noted that research has distinguished between victims of incest and victims of other sexual abuse regarding expression of the distress, fear of harm to a family member, and the existing taboo on the issue. The ambiguity and secrecy surrounding the abuse not only cause a sense of personal guilt, but often a sense of being a partner to the criminal act. Sexual abuse affects the child's development and can sometimes lead to symptoms such as eating disorders, addictions, suicidal tendencies, and other psychological problems.

Post-traumatic Stress Disorder (PTSD) is a disorder in which an ongoing stress response is generated in a victim of a traumatic event, with symptoms including "invasive symptoms," that is, symptoms appearing in the victim's psyche, primarily during sleep, in either nightmares or other dreams.

MEMORY WARS

Memory is one of the most important abilities of living creatures. This capacity allows one to use the stored information that has been acquired via the senses and via knowledge. In this process, neurons transmit electric signals from one to another, with the complexity of the information shaping the neurons' participation in transmitting the electric signals. Current science recognizes that there are hundreds of billions of neurons in the human brain that are involved in creating memories.

Amnesia is a disorder known as the "forgetting disease," and it describes partial or full damage to a person's ability to remember, which of course harms the person's day-to-day functioning. Amnesia can be caused by drug overuse or excess alcohol consumption, or can result from certain medical treatments or a blow to the head. Amnesia can also result from prolonged stress, depression, or bodily injury. There are two main types of amnesia: retrograde amnesia, which is forgetting events that took place before the cause of the amnesia; and anterograde amnesia, the inability to remember new events after the cause of the amnesia.

A repressed memory is an experience that cannot be recalled like a regular memory, due to an internal mechanism that fears extreme emotional distress that cannot be processed by the normal tools available to the body and psyche. This internal mechanism prevents the electrical connections required to bring the event into memory, thus diverting it from the person's awareness. Sometimes, following psychological treatment or hypnosis that enable processing and containment, the person can access the repressed memory and bring it into their conscious awareness. Until the 1990s, repressed memories were a treatment template of clinical psychologists trying to locate repressed trauma.

In the 2000s, repressed memory began to penetrate other spheres, including the field of law. Victims of sexual abuse or patients who discovered traumas and sexual abuse began to use those repressed memories to file complaints with the police and demand that the perpetrators be brought to justice.

Not everyone agrees with the theory of repressed memories, with opposition ranging from absolute rejection to reserved acceptance. The scholarly controversy has earned the name of "memory wars," in which each side tries to convince the public that they are right by holding conventions, writing articles for journals, etc.

The opponents hold that the memory in question is not a repressed memory but rather a mistaken or false memory that was reconstructed in an attempt to convince other people by bringing up 'facts' that did not actually take place. The accepted position today, held by various respected institutions outside of Israel, is somewhere in the middle. The American Psychological Association (APA), for example, does not fully accept the idea of repressed memory regarding people who were sexually abused as children, and holds that they remember only a part of what happened to them. The APA explains that there is no final answer regarding repressed memories, and therefore such claims should be accepted with a grain of salt.

THE EVIDENTIARY PROBLEM OF USING A REPRESSED MEMORY

Besides the question of the existence of repressed memories, Israeli evidentiary theory raises an issue in using such memories, which mostly appear during psychological treatment and sometimes in dreams, as legal evidence. Among other things, a piece of evidence must meet three main criteria: admissibility, reliability, and sufficiency (whether it is enough/possible to rely on this piece of evidence alone). The phenomenon of repressed memories cannot be proven empirically on a scientific level, and therefore courts declare that they make no pretensions of being able to rule in the "memory war." However, on the legal level, while the phenomenon of repressed memories is recognized the phenomenon of false or implanted memories is still a disputed topic.

Israeli Supreme Court Judge Yitzhak Amit discusses the tension between a repressed memory and the process of recovering a memory, and the court's ability to make an indictment in such instances:

1. **The purpose of the process.** Did the complainant begin therapy in order to restore memory regarding a certain offense, in which case he may feel pressure to remember details in order to assist the criminal investigation or

the prosecution of the perpetrator of the offense, or did the complainant seek psychological treatment in order to locate the source of the psychological problems or to treat them, in which case there is less fear of him "filling in details?"

2. **Suggestion.** Was the complainant subjected to suggestion by the therapist or by others, and to what extent does the complainant tend to enter into situations of self-suggestion or "hypnosis," which then increases the fear that the complainant will be influenced by suggestion or will "fill in details?"

3. **Documentation or lack of documentation.** Is there documentation and a record by the complainant's therapist that can help the court determine if he was subject to suggestion by the therapist or others?

4. **The therapist's training and professionalism.** Does the complainant's therapist meet the professionally required standards to treat the complainant?

5. **Expert testimony on behalf of the parties.** The court should allow the parties to submit expert opinions with reference to the therapeutic process and the recovery of the complainant's memory.

6. **Existence of supporting evidence.** Is there external evidence that supports the reliability of the repressed memories, such as the abuser's confession or similar

offenses by him; medical records or documentation indicating signs of childhood sexual abuse; real-time documentation or written statements by the victim of the offense, such as a diary or letter; objective testimony of an eyewitness; or a chain of other facts and circumstances that have evidentiary weight and the like? (Case 5582/09 Anon. vs. the State of Israel, handed down on 20 October 2010, ruling 129)

INDICTING ON THE BASIS OF A DREAM

Over the years, the use of a repressed memory or dreams was a passing trend that garnered little respect in Israeli legal evidentiary theory. In 2012, a district court rejected an attempt to indict some-one on the basis of a repressed memory concerning a sexual offense. The court relied on the school of thought that opposed repressed memories, and voiced the concern that a repressed memory might not be original and could be implanted in the complainant . (Case 2326/1, Anon. vs. State of Israel, issued on 15 March 2012)

In 2014, however, the Israeli legal system was shaken up again. Newspaper headlines screamed that a man was indicted on the basis of his daughter's dreams, which she began to dream at age 29. The story concerns Vered, who was recognized as gifted from age 11 but suffered from panic attacks to the point where she dropped out of school. Repeated examinations did not identify the source of the girl's problem, and she was treated with psychiatric medications. At age 22 Vered moved to New York, where she lived for four years. A year after she arrived in New York she began to have dreams in which she remembered sexual acts that her father had perpetrated on her when she was a child. As a result of these dreams, Vered began psychological treatment in New York. Three years later, in

2002, she returned to Israel and filed a complaint with the police against her father, Benny Shmuel.

Since the offenses in Vered's childhood had already passed the statute of limitations, the prosecution charged Benny Shmuel only with the offenses that occurred at the daughter's later ages. The proceedings lasted from 2002 to 2014, when the case was finally completed by the Supreme Court, Case No. 3958/08, Binyamin Shmuel vs. the State of Israel, issued on 10 September 2014.

In the District Court, Vered's father claimed that his daughter's accusations were false, that her claims were due to her psychological problems and her economic interests, taking into account that she had filed a claim against him for 5,000,000 shekels, which at the time of the court's ruling was still pending. Regarding the repressed memory, it was claimed that interpreting the dream as a trigger for delayed recall of the offenses was not coherent and that it could have been a reality that Vered constructed in her dream or that was implanted in her memory through reading and watching television.

The District Court summoned various expert witnesses in addition to witnesses from among her family members and friends. The witnesses for the prosecution claimed that Vered was right regarding her claims of sexual abuse, given that she had symptoms of sexual abuse that are recreated by casual sexual relations and prostitution. In contrast, experts for the defense claimed that it was a false memory. After hearing the evidence, the judges were divided, with Justices Rotlevy and Vardi expressing the majority opinion: that the accused should be indicted for what he had been charged with, against Justice Amsterdam, who held that he should be acquitted due to the fact that the court could not rely solely on the complainant's' testimony and that Vered's testimony required substantial reinforcement. Regarding the claim that the dream and the repressed memory provided only flimsy evidence, the majority opinion of the District Court was that the defense's claim of "implanting" a memory had not been proven and it had not even been clarified whether the defense was claiming that it was a "recycled" memory, a "reconstructed" memory, an "implanted" memory, or a "fake" memory.

The Supreme Court heard the appeal and upheld the precise examination that the District Court had conducted. In addition, they defined preliminary parameters for evaluating the repressed memory and the complainant's interface with the therapist, and whether she was subject to his suggestion or that of other entities. Regarding a repressed memory, the Court asked that the following be evaluated:

1. Whether there is documentation of the complainant's treatment;

2. The therapist's professional qualifications;

3. Expert testimony regarding the therapeutic process and the restoration of the complainant's memory;

4. The question of the existence of external evidence supporting the reliability of the repressed memories.

Another indictment connected to dreams was handed down in 2020. The Supreme Court, sitting as the Criminal Appeals Court, case no. 2487/18, indicted Yeshayahu Rizkal, who served as a rabbi in a Haredi community in Bnei Brak. He had represented himself as a kabbalist and used dreams that were revealed to him in order to commit acts of rape, under false pretenses.

This turning point was not the end of the story. Continuing its trend of viewing a delayed memory as a real claim, the Court rejected the defense lawyer's claim that the accused should be acquitted due to the fact that the memory in question was a repressed memory. The Court ruled that not every delayed or gradual memory was considered to be a repressed memory. Case No. 8805/14, Zalman Cohen vs. the State of Israel et al, handed down on 7 January 2016; Case No. 1647/17 Anon. vs. the State of Israel et al, handed down on 9 January 2019.

10

CONCLUSION

*"Great dreams are the foundation of the world. [...] The coarseness
of social life being immersed only in its material side, takes the light
of the dream from the world, the glow of its expansion, its supreme
ascension, from the gloomy reality, until the world flutters in pain
from the venomous stings of reality, lacking the glow of the dream.
[...] while only the free dream, rebelling against reality and its
limits, is really the more essential truth of reality."*

Rabbi Abraham Isaac Kook,
Shmoneh Kvatzim (3, 126)

Dreams do not end. Over the course of our lives, we dream many
different dreams, corresponding to the transformations that we
undergo. A youth's dream is not like that of a young father, which in
its turn is unlike that of an elderly woman or a young girl. And yet,
all the dreams go on filling our lives. They breathe hope, future, fears,
and nightmares, and often leave us amazed upon awakening. Some
dreams are cancelled in one fell swoop by the saying, "They tell

false dreams," while others attach a question mark to the saying and wish for the dream's fulfillment. Many of those on whom a dream left its mark will conduct an internet search for information on the meaning of a symbol they saw in their dream.

One cannot be indifferent to dreams, despite the fact that we forget most of them almost immediately. Even though we are accustomed to them, we are still obligated to focus on them and think about them. Throughout the book, I have written about the research that I myself have done, when I suddenly discovered that I don't know enough about the dreams that accompany *me* every night. Like any intellectual journey, and as part of the educational foundations that I inherited from my parents, I understood that this journey must pass through many places: science, philosophy, psychology, the Bible, kabbalah, the Talmud, and the paths of Halacha. Only after I had listened attentively to everything, after I had investigated and read, did I decide to come to rest with this summary.

The journey is not over. Sleep labs and the halls of academia are still saturated with plans and ideas for perfecting and upgrading dreams. Many among us suffer during our dreams and need healing. The Houses of Study weave unique combinations of *pshat* and *sod* [the literal meaning of the text and the mystical meaning], *drash* and *remez* [the aggadic meaning and the allegorical meaning], seeking unique layers that Judaism can contribute to the research on dreams.

Many dreams change the world. Dreamers establish and innovate, create and destroy in response to dreams, even though their origins are unclear and their reliability is in doubt. Therefore dreams will continue, and dreamers will continue in their pursuit. We can only look on with wonder at the event that we experience nightly, and which occupies a significant portion of our lives, but is still shrouded in mystery.

ABOUT THE AUTHOR

Shlomo Yakobovits is an author, litigator, and creative multidisciplinary researcher who combines the vast knowledge he has accumulated in his works. Dr. Yakobovits holds five academic degrees, has authored three books on law, genetics, and workers' rights, manages a law firm, is a certified rabbi, and more.

In the edition of his book created for North American readers, Dr. Yakobovits presents a holistic, up-to-date perspective on dreams through the worlds of science, psychology, philosophy, law, and religion. In simple language, he allows readers a glimpse into the daily process of dreaming.

www.ingramcontent.com/pod-product-compliance
Lightning Source LLC
Chambersburg PA
CBHW020534270326
41927CB00006B/577